ST.MARY'S UNIVERSITY COLLEGE LIBRARY

A COLLEGE OF THE QUEENS UNIVERSITY OF BELFAST

Tel: 028 90327678   Web Site: www.stmarys-belfast.ac.uk   email: library@stmarys-belfast.ac.uk

Fines will be charged for overdue and recalled books not returned by stated date.

Date Due	Date Due	Date Due
14 NOV 2003		
.- 4 JAN 2005		
- 5 APR 2005		
25 APR 2007		
13 JAN 2009		

OTHER BOOKS IN THE SERIES

The Enlargement of the European Union
GRAHAM AVERY AND FRASER CAMERON

Paying for Europe
IAIN BEGG AND NIGEL GRIMWADE

Democracy in the European Union
CHRISTOPHER LORD

The Politics of European Union Regional Policy

Multi-Level Governance or Flexible Gatekeeping?

Ian Bache

Published by
Sheffield Academic Press Ltd
Mansion House
19 Kingfield Road
Sheffield S11 9AS
England

Typeset by Sheffield Academic Press
and
Printed on acid-free paper in Great Britain
by Cromwell Press
Trowbridge, Wiltshire

British Library Cataloguing in Publication Data

A catalogue record for this book is available
from the British Library

ISBN 1-85075-863-8

Contents

List of Tables

Series Foreword

This is the third publication in a new series—Contemporary European Studies—created through the collaboration between Sheffield Academic Press and the University Association for Contemporary European Studies (UACES).

For over 25 years UACES has been the leading organization in bringing together academics and practitioners from a variety of disciplines concerned with the study of contemporary Europe. The emphasis of the Association's activities has been that of European integration and it has been increasingly concerned with the institutions and policies of the European Union. Contemporary European Studies will reflect those interests and will also respond to the needs of those studying contemporary Europe by providing authoritative texts on a range of issues in this area, with the emphasis on the European Union. It is my intention, as series editor, to make sure that the four publications a year in this series include a balance covering the theoretical and policy issues as well as the internal and external concerns of the EU. In establishing the series, UACES also wanted the series to include promising younger authors, as well as the more established names.

Ian Bache comes under the former heading. He is a Lecturer in the Department of Politics at the University of Sheffield who has translated his expert knowledge of the structural funds of the European Union into a form that is accessible both for students of the European Union and those who teach courses on it. This book describes the funds and their importance within the EU, and examines the politics of structural funds both within the EU and within Member States.

I am grateful to Mrs Jean Allen of Sheffield Academic Press for her assistance not only in the production of this book but for her ready support for the series. I would also like to thank the members of the series' editorial committee, Professor Stephen George and Judy Batt, for their help with the series.

Clive Archer
Series Editor

Acknowledgments

This book draws on various pieces of work completed both as a postgraduate and as a member of staff at the Department of Politics, University of Sheffield. During this time I have accumulated a number of debts. Two people have been particularly important. Stephen George, first as my PhD supervisor and later as a colleague and collaborator, has been an invaluable source of advice and encouragement. Linda McAvan, as a friend and former colleague, has supplied both support and insight. To both of them I am extremely grateful.

In addition I would like to thank the numerous policy-makers, politicians and others who have generously given their time to be interviewed for the various projects feeding into this book. The Economic and Social Research Council has been an important source of funding over this period, most recently through research grant no. R000222447.

For their comments on an earlier draft of this book I would like to express my gratitude to Harvey Armstrong, Stephen George, James Mitchell, Joanne Scott, Maria Tofarides and Peter Wells. All the usual disclaimers apply. Finally, I would like to thank my family for their continued encouragement.

This book is dedicated to two special people: my wife Pamela and my son Thomas. In their different ways, both have been crucial in allowing me to complete this book.

Ian Bache

Abbreviations

BCA	Basic Credit Approval
CAP	Common Agricultural Policy
CED	Community Economic Development
CEEC	Central and East European countries
CI	Community Initiative
COREPER	Committee of Permanent Representatives
CSF	Community Support Framework
CURDS	Centre for Urban and Regional Development Studies
DG	Directorate General
DoE	(UK) Department of the Environment
DTI	(UK) Department of Trade and Industry
EAGGF	European Agricultural Guarantee and Guidance Fund
EC	European Community
ECSC	European Coal and Steel Community
ECU	European Currency Unit
EEC	European Economic Community
EIB	European Investment Bank
EMU	economic and monetary union
ERDF	European Regional Development Fund
ESF	European Social Fund
EU	European Union
EU15	European Union of 15 Member States
EURACOM	European Action for Mining Communities
Euratom	European Atomic Energy Community
FIFG	Financial Instrument of Fisheries Guidance
GDP	Gross Domestic Product
GDR	German Democratic Republic
GNP	Gross National Product
IMP	Integrated Mediterranean Programme
IR	international relations
LI	liberal intergovernmentalism
MLG	multi-level governance
MSC	Manpower Service Commission
MUA	Million Units of Account

NIERC	Northern Ireland Economic Research Council
OPEC	Organization of Petroleum-Exporting Countries
RDF	Regional Development Fund (see also ERDF)
RDP	Regional Development Plan
RECHAR	Community initiative programme for the conversion of coal mining areas
RENAVAL	Community initiative programme for the conversion of shipbuilding areas
RESIDER	Community initiative programme for the conversion of steel areas
SCA	Supplementary Credit Approval
SEA	Single European Act
SEM	Single European Market
SPD	single programming document

Introduction

EC or EU?

While it has become a commonplace to refer in general to *EU* policies, it is more precise to refer to regional policy as an *EC* policy. Regional policy falls under the European Community (social and economic) 'pillar' of the European Union (the other two pillars being Justice and Home Affairs and Common Foreign and Security Policy). The 'EU' is the term for describing the collectivity of Member States belonging to the Union and will be used as such where appropriate. In relation to regional policy, 'EC' is the preferred term here unless it is more accurate historically to refer to the EEC or Common Market.

Regional Policy

A problem of writing a book on the politics of EC regional policy is that of defining its coverage. To take the subject of regional policy first, its content is less obvious than it might first appear. McAleavey (1995a: 10-11) provides a helpful point of departure:

> The *core principle* of regional development policy in general is that there is a role for the public sector, on economic and social grounds, to intervene in the market to reduce spatial economic disparities which arise as a consequence of market forces. In other words, there is a role for government in attempting to influence the geographical distribution of economic activity (McAleavey 1995a: 10-11; emphasis original).

While this definition is straightforward, a confusing number of terms has arisen to describe EC activities related to this objective: 'regional policy', 'structural policy' and 'cohesion policy' are the most common. These terms are often used interchangeably to describe a range of measures. This section will explain these terms and say why the preferred term is '*regional* policy'.

This book focuses on the main *financial* instrument of EC *regional policy*, the European Regional Development Fund (ERDF), which was created in 1975. However, other EC financial instruments have regional aspects. Of particular importance are the European Social Fund (ESF) and the 'Guidance' section of the European Agricultural Guidance and Guarantee Fund (EAGGF). Since 1988, the ERDF, ESF and EAGGF collectively have been known as the *structural funds*, informed by *structural policy*. In 1993, the Financial Instrument of Fisheries Guidance (FIFG) was added to the structural funds. Within the structural funds, the ERDF has remained the largest and most important instrument of regional policy. To complicate the picture further, the term *cohesion policy* came into use after the Single European Act of 1986 to describe a range of Community measures, including the structural funds, aimed at reducing economic and social disparities in Europe. The main non-structural fund instrument was the Cohesion Fund, introduced in 1993. This fund was not subject to the structural policy agreements that governed the operation of the structural funds.

The primary focus on ERDF here is not just to simplify the task, although that is important, but also because it is the politics around this aspect of *regional* policy that have arguably been of most interest politically. Other aspects of regional policy, such as control of national state aids, are not a prominent feature of this book. Thus the term 'regional policy' is generally used as shorthand for the principles guiding ERDF, but the terms 'structural policy' and 'cohesion policy' are used where it is more accurate.

The *Politics* of Regional Policy

This book provides an overview of the key developments in the politics of EC regional policy. The key concern of the book is to consider the issue of political influence in relation to regional policy; in other words, the question of *who decides what and to what effect*. The first part of this question is regularly addressed in studies of EU policy-making; the second part less so. It is a contention of this book that most attempts at understanding policy-making in the EU have focused on the politics of initial decision-making at EU level—the 'who decides what' question—and neglected the importance of policy implementation within domestic arenas, where the 'effect' of policies can be measured. The argument here is that to understand the *real* influence of various actors requires understanding of the significance of policy decisions as they affect policy *outcomes*.

The Structure of the Book

I begin by discussing key theoretical perspectives developed to explain policy-making in the EU. From this discussion, a framework of analysis is developed to guide reading of subsequent chapters. The empirical material presented is then discussed in relation to the theoretical arguments presented in Chapter 1. In the empirical material, the UK features heavily, which reflects the importance of the UK to the creation and development of EC regional policy. From a number of analytical perspectives and at different stages of the policy process, the UK provides an ideal case study.

Chapter 1 outlines developments in theoretical explanations of EU policy-making, from the 'traditional' theories of neofunctionalism and intergovernmentalism to the contemporary theories of multi-level governance and liberal intergovernmentalism. The chapter also discusses the analytical tools of the policy networks approach. From this discussion, the chapter concludes by outlining a framework of analysis to guide reading of subsequent chapters. Chapter 2 traces the development of regional policy from the signing of the Treaty of Rome in 1957 to the creation of the ERDF in 1975. Chapter 3 considers developments in regional policy up to 1988. Chapter 4 discusses the major reform of 'structural policy' in 1988 and the subsequent review in 1993. Chapter 5 looks at the politics of implementation, focusing on the regional policy principles of partnership and additionality. Chapter 6 considers the most recent developments and future prospects for regional policy, including proposals for reform in 1999. Chapter 7 reflects on the utility of the theoretical propositions outlined in Chapter 1 and develops the concept of *flexible gatekeeping* as a counterpoint to the claims of multi-level governance.

1 |

Theoretical Issues

Introduction

No single theory can explain the complex politics of policy-making in the European Union. Moreover, no single chapter could summarize adequately the range of contributions made to understanding these complexities. Instead, this chapter is built on an essentially 'Anglo-American' international relations (IR) debate that has dominated theorizing of the EU until recently. This traditional debate was based on the competing theories of neofunctionalism and intergovernmentalism and more recently was supplanted by the contemporary competing theories of EU policy-making of multi-level governance and liberal intergovernmentalism.

This chapter has five sections. It begins by summarizing 'traditional' competing IR theories of EU policy-making. The second section considers the contribution of the domestic politics approach to understanding EU policy-making. Section 3 looks at contemporary competing theories of EU policy-making in the IR tradition, while Section 4 discusses the application to the EU of an approach developed from the study of domestic politics: policy networks. Finally, the chapter presents a framework of analysis for guiding the reading of subsequent chapters. The concluding chapter of the book reflects on the utility of these approaches to understanding the EU and discusses some recent alternative conceptualizations of policy-making. (For more information on approaches to the studying the EU, see Hix 1994; Caporaso and Keeler 1995; Risse-Kappen 1996; Wallace and Wallace 1996).

'Traditional' Competing Theories of EU Policy-Making

Early attempts to explain developments in the European Union were concerned with the nature and pace of integration between nation-states. These explanations came from international relations. Initially,

IR theories of European integration were adapted to study developments in specific policy sectors. Subsequently, the study of the EU shifted partly from an IR focus on politics 'among' nations to a focus on politics 'within' the new EU system of governance (Hix 1994: 23). Yet the starting point for understanding theoretical developments in the study of the EU is with IR.

Historically, two competing theories emanating from IR dominated the debate over developments in European integration: realists applied *intergovernmentalism* (Hoffmann 1964, 1966) and pluralists developed *neofunctionalism* (Haas 1958; Lindberg 1963). Intergovernmentalists argued that national governments determined the nature and pace of integration and acted as 'gatekeepers' between supranational developments and their domestic systems (Hoffmann 1966). As such, intergovernmental cooperation within the EU was not significantly different from that in other international regimes. In contrast, neofunctionalists insisted that each integrative step led logically to another and governments would increasingly find themselves unable to resist the pressures for integration. Supranational and subnational actors would become increasingly influential. (For an overview, see Caporaso and Keeler 1995; George 1996; Risse-Kappen 1996).

Neofunctionalism
In the first period of European integration following the signing of the Treaty of Rome in 1957, neofunctionalism appeared to be winning the theoretical debate. Neofunctionalism sought to explain 'how and why they (states) voluntarily mingle, merge and mix with their neighbours so as to lose the factual attributes of sovereignty while acquiring new techniques for resolving conflict between themselves' (Haas 1970: 610). Of particular importance to the neofunctionalist explanation of change in relations between states in Europe was the predictive concept of 'spillover'. Two types of spillover were important to early neofunctionalist writers: functional and political. The first was based on the understanding that modern industrial economies were made up of interconnected parts and, if Member States integrated one functional sector of their economies, technical pressures would prompt integration in related sectors.

Political spillover involved the build-up of political pressures in favour of further integration within the states involved. Once one sector of the economy was integrated, nationally based interest groups operating in that sector would rapidly come to appreciate the benefits available to them as a result of integration. These groups would then lobby their own governments to support further integration. Other interest groups, aware of advantages accruing to their counterparts in the integrated sector, would also become advocates of integration and the pressures on national governments would become overwhelming.

A third type of spillover was added by later theorists to explain the part played by the Commission in fostering integration. 'Cultivated' spillover referred to the expectation that the Commission, and other supranational actors, would encourage the development of EC-wide pressure groups and also cultivate contacts with national interest groups and national civil servants. These groups and individuals would be potential Commission allies in conflicts with national governments (see Tranholm-Mikkelsen 1991).

In short, neofunctionalists argued that, once national governments took the initial steps towards integration, the process took on a life of its own and swept governments along further than they anticipated going. Eventually, this process would lead to an end condition resembling some form of federal European state.

In the 1950s, the theory neatly fitted events, particularly in explaining the transition from the ECSC to the EC. Yet the theory was not exclusively predictive: it had a normative element that was seized on by advocates of a federal Europe. Commission officials and members saw neofunctionalist writings as a blueprint for advancing integration. The beginning of the end for neofunctionalist theory in its original manifestation came in the early 1960s and in particular the use of the veto by de Gaulle, leading to the 'empty chair' crisis of 1965–66. National governments had power and were clearly prepared to use it to determine the nature and pace of integration:

> By 1967 Haas was already attempting to cope with the possibility that de Gaulle had 'killed the Common Market' by revising his theory to account for the prospect of 'disintegration', and by 1975 he was announcing the 'obsolescence of regional integration theory' (Caporaso and Keeler 1995: 36-37).

Intergovernmentalism

Hoffmann's intergovernmentalism was the main response to neofunctionalism. He argued that neofunctionalism followed the logic of a blender, 'which crunches the most diverse products, overcomes their different tastes and perfumes, and replaces them with one, presumably delicious juice' (1966: 882). By way of contrast, Hoffmann emphasized the logic of diversity. He argued that 'in areas of key importance to the national interest, nations prefer the certainty, or the self-controlled uncertainty of national self-reliance, to the uncontrolled uncertainty of the untested blender' (Hoffmann 1966: 882). In short, where an issue was considered important enough, national governments would be effective gatekeepers, protecting and promoting their policy preferences.

Hoffmann acknowledged that other actors and interests played a role in the process of integration, but viewed national governments as the ultimate arbiters of key decisions. He refuted the neofunctionalist argument that their decisions were not explainable only in terms of pressure from organized interests, arguing that often 'political calculations lead governments to take positions to which powerful groups are hostile' (1964: 93). These political calculations were driven by domestic concerns. In particular, the impact of integrative decisions on the national economy and on the electoral prospects of the party in government. Later scholars developed the importance of domestic politics to decisions affecting European integration more fully (see below).

Hoffmann's portrayal of national governments as gatekeepers provoked strong criticism. Carol Webb argued that

> the overdrawn, unidimensional image of national governments favoured by intergovernmentalists is inadequate and distorting. Far from being efficient and effective gatekeepers straddling the threshold between their national boundaries and the Community, national governments more closely resemble the juggler who must apply himself simultaneously to the tasks of keeping several balls in the air and not losing his balance on the rotating platform (1983: 32).

Moreover, the early under-theorization of domestic politics in shaping national government negotiating positions prompted further criticisms of the early intergovernmentalist position:

> Governments have to construct policy packages which both adequately represent domestic claims and yet can, nevertheless, be used as an effective bargaining counter in Brussels. What emerges in many instances... is something less than a consistently highly orchestrated and impenetrable national front (Webb 1983: 24-25).

Such criticisms undermined the intergovernmentalist reliance on the realist concept of governments acting in the national interest. In terms of EU negotiations, it was clear that, while governments would assert their right to defend the national interest, this was often 'a substitute for the articulation of partisan preferences' (H. Wallace 1977a: 47).

The Domestic Politics Approach

Perhaps the most significant discussion of domestic politics and EU decision-making came from Simon Bulmer (1983). However, this was not the first contribution to this debate. In particular, Helen Wallace (1977a) drew attention to the importance of different administrative traditions and political objectives of Member States in formulating positions on 'Community' issues. These differences produced variations in the coherence of national positions at EU level. Britain and France, for example, were identified as having centralized administrative systems which had, in principle 'permitted these governments to identify a relatively consistent line in Community negotiations' (H. Wallace 1977a: 48). While a centralized administrative system may have facilitated a more consistent negotiating position for these governments, this did not necessarily reflect a domestic consensus on issues.

Wallace identified a number of other factors as important in shaping the national response to Community issues:

> the quality and morale of the national civil services, the internal balance of each government, and the constitutional role of their political leaders ... The differential weights of particular ministries and their client groups in each national process are relevant—the strength of the British Treasury and Foreign Office (H. Wallace 1977a: 48).

Bulmer (1983) made a number of important points to inform then-contemporary theories. First and foremost, Bulmer argued that existing theories failed to provide an analytical framework for structuring the impact of domestic politics on the EC. There had been too much focus on the 'upper tier' of EC policy-making—the formal institutional framework of the Communities—without examining the domestic sources of national negotiating positions. Secondly, Bulmer argued that EC policy-making processes did not follow the logic of integration, but that integration followed the logic of policy-making processes. These processes had their roots in the power structures of the nation-states.

Bulmer suggested that neofunctionalism placed too much emphasis on the role of interest groups and other elites in maintaining the momentum of integration. Further, while recognizing the centrality of national governments, intergovernmentalism was seen to offer little for the purposes of analysing Member States' attitudes towards the EC. It tended to view national governments as omnipotent, monolithic structures when no evidence was presented to support this assumption. In contrast, Bulmer argued that EC policy is formulated differently in different Member States. Whether policy is decided through consensus or imposition depends on national political culture, and the government's strength along with the strength of interest groups, parliamentary bodies, political parties and subnational government.

From his criticism of existing theories, Bulmer outlined a number of key assumptions of the domestic politics approach:

- the national polity is the basic unit in the EC;

- each national polity has a different set of social and economic conditions that shapes its national interests and policy content;

- European policy only represents one facet of a national polity's activity; in formal terms the national governments hold a key position at the junction of national politics and Community politics;

- the concept of policy style is employed to analyse the relationships between governments and other domestic political forces vis-à-vis European policy.

In summary, Bulmer's approach was essentially a call for existing theories to be less glib in their treatment of domestic politics. Its purpose was to add to the understanding of the complex nature of policy-making in the EC and made no claim to explain policy-making from an overall EC perspective. The challenge to intergovernmentalists posed by the domestic politics approach was later taken up by Andrew Moravcsik (1991, 1993) in a reformulation of intergovernmentalism. Around the same time, Gary Marks (1992, 1993) followed renewed interest in neofunctionalism in the late 1980s with a revised pluralist approach to understanding the European Union.

Contemporary Competing Theories of the EU Policy-Making

The launch of the single market programme in 1985, signalling a new phase in European integration, was quickly followed by new theoretical developments in both the pluralist and realist traditions. In the pluralist tradition, Gary Marks (1992, 1993) developed the concept of 'multi-level governance' (MLG) to describe how the EU was moving towards a system of decision-making in which power was shared across multiple levels of government: subnational, national and supranational. In contrast, Andrew Moravcsik (1993) and Mark Pollack (1995), among others, continued to emphasize the role played by national governments. In particular, Moravcsik (1993) accounted for earlier critiques by accommodating a pluralist explanation of domestic foreign policy formation in his model of *liberal* intergovernmentalism (LI). At the centre of the debate remained the Commission's ability to advance integrative measures that conflicted with the policy preferences of national governments. In this revived debate, and in the work on multi-level governance in particular, 'structural' policy was a key area of discussion.

Multi-Level Governance
At the core of multi-level governance is the argument that collective decision-making and the independent role of supranational institutions are eroding the sovereignty of national governments in Europe. In addition, governments are less able to control the activities of other domestic actors on the international stage. In other words: 'European integration is a polity creating process in which authority and policy-making influence are shared across multiple levels of government— subnational, national and supranational' (Marks *et al.* 1996: 342).

Yet the MLG model does not deny that national governments 'remain the most important pieces of the European puzzle' (Marks *et al.* 1996: 346). At the same time, Marks (1996b) is critical of the inter-governmentalist conception of the 'state' as an actor in international relations. He distinguishes between the state as a set of institutional rules and the state as a reference to political actors. In this conception, 'institutions do not think, have preferences or act, but are sets of commonly accepted formal and informal norms that constrain political actors (i.e., individuals and groups of individuals) who are the only agents capable of goal-orientated action' (Marks 1996b: 5). To explain how the national state can be weakened in both the international and domestic arenas, Marks developed the *actor-centred* approach. Here the focus is not on whole states or national governments as key players, but on those individuals who are in key positions of authority in national governments—elected party leaders—whose goals are not limited simply to defending central state competencies (Marks 1996a: 8).

Marks posits three distinct situations in which national political actors either concede authority willingly or are pressured to do so. First, because it is politically advantageous to do so; secondly, because some other concern outweighs their resistance; and, thirdly, because government leaders are unable to check or reverse the dispersal of authority to subnational or supranational leaders (Marks 1996b). It is this third scenario that places MLG firmly in the neofunctionalist tradition and in conflict with contemporary intergovernmentalism, although Marks (1993: 407) rejects both approaches as 'too narrow' in failing to account for the 'mobilization and empowerment of subnational governments'.

In terms of 'structural policy', Marks identified three distinct phases of decision-making: bargaining the financial envelope, creating the institutional context, and structural programming: 'The first concerns decisions over financial redistribution; the second concerns how funds should be administered, the 'institutional context'; and the third is concerned with the operationalization of CSFs' (Marks 1996a: 389-406). Marks made further distinctions at the level of implementation or 'structural programming'. These were: (1) the formulation of national or, more commonly, regional development plans that become the basis of negotiation with the Commission; (2) the transformation of regional development plans into formal contracts allocating resources (CSFs); (3) the negotiation of CSFs into Operational Programmes, which detail the projects to be funded to achieve CSF priorities; and (4) the implementation and monitoring of Operational Programmes (Marks 1996a: 398-406).

In the terms specified by the advocates of multi-level governance, there would appear to be no better case study of the model than the implementation of EC regional policy. This is for two reasons. First, that regional policy is considered to be at 'the leading edge of multi-level governance in which supranational, national, regional, and local governments are enmeshed in territorially overarching policy networks' (Marks 1993: 402-403). And secondly, that 'Multi-level governance is prominent in the implementation stage' (Marks, Hooghe and Blank 1996: 365). This argument will be revisited in the concluding chapter.

Liberal Intergovernmentalism
Following traditional realism, Moravcsik's liberal intergovernmental approach assumed that states were rational actors, but departed from

traditional realism in its emphasis on the domestic process of foreign policy formation. According to Moravcsik (1995: 613), LI has a 'basic tripartite structure' of foreign policy preference formation, inter-state bargaining and institutional delegation. The first part involves a pluralistic domestic process that determines each state's definition of the national interest and thus the position that governments take with them into the international negotiation. The second part of the analysis is to see how conflicting national interests are reconciled in the negotiating forum of the Council of Ministers. The third part seeks to explain the circumstances under which governments delegate powers to supra-national institutions. While this tripartite structure does not itself comprise a theory, it has

> intrinsic theoretical content, since it is based on various assumptions, e.g. governments are the fundamental actors, they act in an instrumental fashion, and, therefore, the formation of preferences analytically (though not always temporally) precedes bargaining, which in turn precedes delegation (Moravcsik 1995: 613).

Moravcsik's basic assumption was that the EC could be explained with reference to general theories of international relations, as an example of a successful international regime. In such a regime, the behaviour of states reflected the rational actions of governments constrained at home by societal pressures and abroad by their strategic environment. Essentially, Moravcsik reasserted the basic claims of realism, while accepting the validity of some of the criticisms made of it. His position took on board some of the issues raised by neofunctionalism, and by the wider pluralist perspective of which it was a part.

For example, Moravcsik states that 'it would be absurd to assume… that supranational officials do not matter in daily decisions, since Member States often expressly delegate power to them and, moreover, do so under conditions of imperfect information and uncertainty' (Moravcsik 1995: 612). However, while delegated powers give supra-national actors scope for influencing decisions, Moravcsik maintains that '*intergovernmental demand* for policy ideas, not the *supranational supply* of those ideas, is the fundamental exogenous factor driving integration. To a very large extent, the demand for cooperative policies creates its own supply' (1995: 618; emphasis original).

So, for Moravcsik, the governments of states remain the dominant actors and 'the influence of supranational actors is generally marginal, limited to situations where they have strong domestic allies' (1995:

612). Yet he acknowledged, in response to criticism by Daniel Wincott (1995), that LI could not account for all aspects of European integration. In particular, LI needed further development to explain 'the complex issues that arise when power is delegated to supranational actors under conditions of imperfect information and uncertainty' (Moravcsik 1995: 611).

The Policy Networks Approach

> ...the partial or incomplete coverage of European institutions makes the rules of access to the institutions very unclear and more unclear than in most established polities...It is partly for this reason that 'policy networks' currently amongst the most attractive and rewarding areas of study have become so important (Wallace and Wallace 1996: 27).

Theorists have long recognized that policy-making in the European Union is complex, varying across policy sectors and over time, 'depending on the extent of Community involvement, the type of instruments used, and the continuing importance of national policies' (H. Wallace 1983a: 52). The problem of theorizing EU policy-making is complicated further by the argument that the policy process is not confined to what happens within the formal framework of EU institutions, but also '...embraces a network of relationships and contacts among national policy-makers in the different member states, both directly through involvement in the Community arena and indirectly as that arena impinges on national policy processes' (H. Wallace 1977a: 33-34).

Finally, policy-making theories have to account for the influence of various governmental and non-governmental actors at different stages in the policy process. In particular, it is necessary at a minimum to distinguish between decision-making at EU level and the policy implementation stage, which is in practice a national matter. Theories from IR have largely ignored this distinction. Multi-level governance has highlighted the distinction, but the importance of implementation remains a largely under-researched aspect of EU policy-making.

The policy networks approach was developed as a model of interest group intermediation in domestic politics. It was a response to the failure of existing pluralist and corporatist explanations in accounting for variations in government–interest group relations in different policy sectors. The response was a disaggregated approach to policy analysis which argued that 'in most policy areas a limited number of interests are involved in the policy-making process' and that 'many fields are characterised by continuity, not necessarily as far as policy outcomes is concerned, but in terms of the groups involved in policy-making' (Rhodes and Marsh 1992: 4).

The Rhodes Model

R.A.W. Rhodes (1981) developed the policy networks model, which was subsequently applied to the study of the EU by Peterson (1992, 1995a) and others. According to the Rhodes model, a policy network is a set of resource-dependent organizations. Networks have different structures of dependencies that vary along five key dimensions: the constellation of interests; membership; vertical interdependence; horizontal interdependence; and the distribution of resources (Rhodes 1988: 77-8).

Rhodes (1988) distinguished between five different types of network ranging from highly integrated policy communities to loosely integrated issue networks. Between these, on what is seen as a continuum, are professional networks, intergovernmental networks and producer networks, respectively. At one end of the continuum, policy communities are characterized by

> stability of relationships, continuity of a highly restrictive membership, vertical interdependence based on shared service delivery responsibilities and insulation from other networks and invariably from the general public (including Parliament). They have a high degree of vertical interdependence and limited horizontal articulation (Rhodes 1988: 78).

At the other end of the continuum, issue networks are distinguished by their large number of participants and limited degree of interdependence. The structure tends to be atomistic and stability and continuity are 'at a premium' (Rhodes 1988: 78).

In applying the Rhodes model to the study of the EU, Peterson (1995a) distinguished between super-systemic and systemic levels of decision making at EU-level. The *super-systemic level* is concerned with history-making decisions, usually taken at EU summits by the European Council, which transcend the EU's ordinary policy process: 'History-making decisions alter the Union's legislative procedures, rebalance the relative powers of European Union institutions, or change the EU's remit' (Peterson 1995a: 72). *Systemic decision-making*, on the other hand, is concerned with policy-setting decisions, where choices are made between alternative courses of action according to one of several versions of the 'Community method' of decision-making' (Peterson: 1995a: 73). The dominant actor at this level is the Council of Ministers, although less controversial matters are dealt with by national civil servants working together through the Committee of Permanent Representatives (COREPER).

Power Dependence

Organizations within networks are interdependent: each organization is dependent on others for certain resources—financial, informational, political, organizational or constitutional-legal—and it is the extent to which an organization controls and can mobilize these resources that determines its power in a given situation. These 'resource dependencies' are the key variable in shaping policy outcomes. As Peterson and Bomberg (1993: 28) put it, 'They set the "chessboard" where private and public interests manoeuvre for advantage.' However, interdependence is 'almost always asymmetrical' and in some cases it is possible to talk of 'unilateral leadership' within networks (Rhodes 1986b: 5).

A particular strength of the policy networks approach is its emphasis on policy implementation, which Rhodes described as: 'a process of bargaining between conflicting interests. Policy does not 'fail' but is actually made in the course of negotiations between the (ostensible) implementers' (Rhodes 1986a:14). Implementation can be a crucial phase in the policy-making process and cannot be seen simply as a straightforward administrative follow-on. Barrett and Hill (1986: 5) stated:

> The political processes by which policy is mediated, negotiated and modified during its formulation and legitimation do not stop when initial policy decisions have been made, but continue to influence policy through the behaviour of those affected by policy acting to protect or enhance their own interests.

The importance of policy implementation has been long established in studies of domestic policies, but relatively neglected in the study of the EU.

The Importance of Implementation

> For rather obvious reasons, the initial decision to do something seems to be the most important part of policy-making. The awareness has grown, however, that the initial objectives can be substantially transformed as they are put into practice (Rhodes 1986a: 101).

The problem for the European Commission in securing policy objectives agreed at EU level is its dependence on national administrative systems for policy implementation. These systems are invariably closely linked to the authority of national governments. Thus, the implementation stage of EU policy-making can offer national governments considerable scope for shaping policy outcomes. Where the system of government in a Member State is highly centralized, the scope for national government influence within the domestic networks is that much greater.

At the same time, however, the implementation stage of EU policy-making broadens considerably the number of actors involved in the policy process so that the nature of conflict over policy may change and new tensions may arise. Thus, the involvement of new actors at the implementation stage may also present new opportunities for the Commission. In short:

> it is only by examining the implementation phases that we can begin to gauge the effectiveness of Community policies in relation to the objectives sought, or to assess whether the experience of member governments and other national agencies at this stage increases or decreases their support for an extension of Community activity (H. Wallace 1977a: 57).

While this argument has long been stated, detailed studies of the *political* aspects of EU policy implementation have been relatively scarce (McAleavey 1995a: 136). The increased application of the policy networks approach may go some way to correcting this.

Concluding Remarks

While the policy networks approach can help explain policy-making in the EU, it does not constitute a predictive theory. Its scope is restricted to providing 'tools' for analysing links between types of governmental units, between levels of government, and between governments and interest groups. As Peterson and Bomberg (1993: 31) argued:

> Policy networks are essentially descriptive theoretical tools which simply help order facts and evidence in novel ways. However, policy networks can be used to anticipate and explain policy outputs by providing insights into how and why decisions were taken which produced them.

Importantly, the policy networks approach emphasizes the analysis of links between actors at all stages of the policy process, including implementation, to explain policy-making.

Conclusion

This chapter has summarized some of the main theoretical debates over the nature of decision-making in the EU. The focus has been on the parts of the contributions most relevant to an examination of regional policy. There has been no attempt to mislead in this endeavour, but some important omissions are inevitable. During the period of theoretical development sketched above, the EC has moved from being an emergent system to one that has a defined institutional structure. As such, the concern of academics has turned, to an extent, away from explaining emergent structures and towards examining the political process within those structures. As Caporaso and Keeler (1995: 56) put it: 'Politics and policymaking within institutions have assumed an analytical place alongside the politics of institutional change.'

From this brief discussion of theoretical contributions to the understanding of decision-making in the EU, it is possible to outline a framework to guide the reading of this book. For conceptual purposes, this framework refers to factors *above*, *within* and *below* the EU system. In reality, these distinctions are blurred and what is most important are the linkages between these conceptually distinct levels of decision-making.

1. Factors 'above' or 'external' to the EU system are important in shaping EU level decisions. Changes in the international economy are particularly important.

2. Factors 'below' EU level exchanges, in penetrated domestic arenas, shape EU level decisions over regional policy.

3. 'Within' or 'internal to' the political system of the EU, decisions are contested by national, supranational and subnational actors. It may be useful to subdivide decision-making stages at EU level, both to understand related decisions within a policy sector and linkages across policy sectors.

4. Implementation is an important stage in the regional policy process in which EU level objectives can be frustrated. It may be useful to subdivide decision-making at the policy implementation stage.

5. 'Non-state' actors exercise influence over EU level decisions and over policy implementation to varying degrees.

While most commentators would accept that each of these points has validity, scholars working in different traditions place different emphasis on the importance of different actors and different levels of decision-making.

Early contributions to the theoretical debate are considered in the chapters on the creation and early development of regional policy. The book then turns to the contemporary debate over policy-making in the EU. At the leading edge of this debate is the work on multi-level governance, developed through a study of 'structural' policy. The proponents of liberal intergovernmentalism question this framework. Both the 'traditional' and 'new' competing theories raise important questions about the nature of policy-making in the EU. Developments in regional policy have been at the centre of this debate. To consider the above questions, the remainder of the book proceeds through a discussion of the creation, development and implementation of EC regional policy to the present day.

2 |

The Creation of EC Regional Policy

Introduction

This chapter looks at developments on the road to the creation of EC
regional policy in 1975. It begins with a brief discussion of EC financial instruments with a regional dimension prior to the creation of the
main financial instrument of regional policy, the European Regional
Development Fund (ERDF). The chapter then considers the origins of
the ERDF and the negotiations over its introduction in 1975. The
importance of domestic politics in the negotiations is illustrated through
the case of the UK. Consideration is then given to some of the implementation issues that arose after 1975. The chapter concludes by
reflecting on the factors that led to the creation of EC regional policy.

The Treaty of Rome and Regional Policy

Awareness of regional economic disparities in Europe has been long
established. In 1958 it was noted that the regional GDP in Hamburg
was five times greater than in Calabria (Halstead 1982: 55). Yet the
Treaty of Rome made no specific commitment to the creation of a
Community regional policy. It did, however, provide a more general
objective of promoting throughout the Community '...a harmonious
development of economic activities, a continuous and balanced expansion' (Article 2). The preamble to the Treaty also made reference to
'reducing the differences between the various regions and the backwardness of the less favoured regions' (Swift 1978: 10). At this stage, it
was not clear whether these disparities would be addressed through
national or Community regional policies, or a combination of both. For
almost two decades, the responsibility remained national.

Yet, while Community regional policy was not introduced until
1975, a number of early financial instruments had a regional dimension:
the European Social Fund (ESF); the European Coal and Steel Commu-

nity (ECSC); the European Investment Bank (EIB); and the European Agricultural Guidance and Guarantee Fund (EAGGF). These are discussed briefly before looking at the main financial instrument of regional policy after 1975, the ERDF.

The European Social Fund
While the Treaty of Rome was framed in the context of a liberal market philosophy, it did include a chapter on social policy. However, this was not its central purpose, and advances in the social field would be linked to progress towards a common market and equal competition between Member States. The European Social Fund was set up by the Treaty of Rome to improve mobility within the labour market, primarily by providing funds for the training and retraining of workers affected by industrial restructuring. The Commission interpreted ambiguities on social policy in the Treaty as an opportunity that provided greater scope for it to act. Despite this, it is well documented that progress on EC social policy has been slow and unsatisfactory from the Commission's position (see Cram 1997: 28-60). However, the ESF has expanded considerably since first being introduced in 1958.

The ESF was established to provide a maximum of 50 per cent towards the cost of eligible schemes, with the possibility of an extra 10 per cent in regions with particularly prolonged problems of unemployment. Initially, 50 per cent of total ESF allocations were committed to alleviating long-term structural unemployment and underemployment in disadvantaged regions. In the first decade of its existence, the main beneficiaries of the ESF were Italian agricultural workers heading for the factories of the north, and workers in the Federal Republic of Germany.

In the first reform of the ESF in 1971, its budget was quadrupled and its coverage extended to include workers in declining industries, women, migrant workers, young people and the 'handicapped'. By 1979, 85 per cent of ESF funding went to regions eligible for ERDF assistance (Halstead 1982: 238). In 1983, ESF priorities became more focused, with 75 per cent of expenditure going to unemployed workers under 25, and 40 per cent of the remainder of ESF earmarked for less favoured regions. (For more detail on the early development of the ESF and social policy more generally, see Cram 1997: 28-60, Laffan 1992: 131-36; Moxon-Browne 1993: 152-62).

Under the Commission presidency of Jacques Delors, social policy was boosted in part by the establishment of the Val Duchesse dialogue with the social partners (employers and trade unions) in 1985 and by the signing of the Single European Act (SEA) in the following year. In the SEA, 'the social, as well as the economic, aspects of cohesion are enshrined as part of the "harmonious development" of the Community' (Laffan 1992: 134). Following the signing of the SEA, emphasis on greater social and economic cohesion prompted a move towards greater integration of the various funds aimed at structural adjustment, including the ESF. This led to the major reform of the structural funds in 1988, including a doubling in allocations to the funds. This reform is dealt with later (Chapter 4).

The European Coal and Steel Community
The Treaty of Paris establishing the ECSC in 1952 in part anticipated the decline of Europe's coal and steel industries. In doing so, the ECSC made grants and loans available to aid the 're-adaptation' and 'reconversion' of workers facing redundancy, resettlement or in need of retraining (Article 2). At the same time, under Article 46 of the Treaty, loans were made available for new investment in the coal and steel industries. In addition, from 1955, the ECSC provided housing subsidies linked with industrial reorganization in the coal and steel sectors. Assistance for housing was also available for particular groups of employees, including migrant workers and workers with 'special skills'.

ECSC finance came from Member State contributions provided by an annual levy on the Community budget and from raising funds on the international capital markets.

The causes and nature of the regional problems in parts of the UK, France, Germany and Belgium made these Member States the major beneficiaries. The ECSC was scheduled to be phased out by 2002 as the Treaty of Paris intended.

The European Investment Bank
The EIB was set up in 1958 by the Treaty of Rome. Article 3 provided for 'the establishment of a European Investment Bank to facilitate the economic expansion of the Community by providing fresh resources'. This recognized the need for a mechanism to transfer capital between rich and poor regions and also to attract capital into the Community from outside. The EIB draws its funds from capital subscriptions by

member governments and from large-scale borrowing on international capital markets. This enables it to pass on loans at a preferential rate to both public and private bodies for assisting economic development in the EC's less prosperous regions. The bank was constituted as a non-profit-making organization overseen by a board of directors drawn from the Member States.

In line with the objective of reducing regional disparities, the EIB's board of governors issued a directive in 1958 stating that the bank 'devote a substantial portion of its resources for the financing of projects likely to contribute to the development of less developed regions' (EIB Review 1958–78, quoted in Halstead 1982: 221). Modernization and conversion schemes in declining industrial areas have been a high priority for EIB loans. This has included aid to finance infrastructure projects—irrigation, water supply and sewerage treatment schemes, and telecommunications—as well as support for small-scale industrial ventures.

Unlike the ERDF, the establishment of the EIB was not politically sensitive. It posed no threat to national government policies, simply adding an additional source of investment at the European level. Moreover, the EIB had a structure and identity separate to that of the Community institutions. So, while Community institutions have been involved in its operations, national governments have not viewed the EIB with the suspicion attached to the development of other Community sources of finance.

The European Agricultural Guidance and Guarantee Fund
The European Agricultural Guidance and Guarantee Fund was agreed in 1962 as part of the Common Agricultural Policy (CAP) package. The guidance section of the EAGGF provides investment aid for a variety of measures to assist less favoured agricultural areas. This includes agricultural product marketing, farm modernization and rural development measures. EAGGF funding has been used in conjunction with other financial instruments to assist agriculture as part of broader regional development strategies.

Regional Instruments without a Regional Policy

Despite the fact that a number of Community financial instruments with regional aspects existed in the 1950s and 1960s, this did not constitute a

Community regional policy. In fact, as one observer stated, these instruments were 'quite as likely to work against each other as together and obviously failed to do anything more than pay lip service to the words of the Treaty' (Swift 1978: 12). Commissioner George Thomson, who was centrally involved in the creation of the ERDF in 1975, went even further in his assessment of existing measures: 'Forms of Community aid, useful and well justified as individual acts of policy, when looked at as a whole...appear to be actually widening the regional gap rather than closing it' (quoted in Swift 1978: 14).

In the 1960s and 1970s, there had been a proliferation of regional policy experiments within Member States. This fact, despite their mixed success, made the question of a more significant Community role over regional policy more controversial. Consequently, it was not until 1973 that the decision was taken to introduce a Community regional policy and not until 1975 that the policy came into operation, with the ERDF as the main instrument. The background to the negotiations over the creation of the ERDF provides a large part of the explanation for the nature of the regional policy that emerged.

The Origins of the ERDF

An appropriate starting point for considering the origins of EC regional policy is 1961, when the Commission convened a conference in Brussels to provide the broad outlines of what a Community approach would be. This started a process of Commission deliberations that resulted in the Commission presenting its first report on regional policy to the Council of Ministers in May 1965. The report called for better information on the Community's problems and the coordination of the range of instruments with a regional impact. This would require more activity on the Commission's part and greater coordination over regional instruments between the Commission and member governments. The timing of this report was unfortunate, coming before the 'Luxembourg Crisis' which resulted in the French government refusing to participate in Council of Ministers meetings for several months. The report was merely noted by the Council.

In 1967, following the merger of the executives of the three European Communities (EEC, ECSC and Euratom) into a single European Commission, a Commission directorate general (DG XVI) for regional policy was established. This directorate general brought together those parts of the Commission of the EEC and the High Authority of the ECSC with responsibility for existing regional measures (Vanhove and Klaassen 1987: 398). This merger provided a new impetus to the development of Community regional policy.

In 1969, the Commission made new regional policy proposals to the Council. These included the creation of a (European) Regional Development Fund, targeted through regional programmes and overseen by a standing committee on regional development made up of national governments and the Commission. The Commission argued that the absence of a policy to address the Community's regional problems undermined the effectiveness of other policies, notably the implementation of economic and monetary union.

Despite a subsequent period of consultation with Member States, there was no significant movement on the Commission's proposals until 1972. Only Italy, potentially the greatest beneficiary from regional measures, was in favour, with the other member governments having different reasons for opposition:

> The French Government wanted to limit Community funding to the EIB, with no role for the Commission. The Belgians would accept no Community policy unless it would endorse its own policy towards internal tensions. The German government favoured only modest regional expenditure restricted to the EAGGF and argued that the principle of redistribution should be *le just retour* (H. Wallace 1977b: 141).

The efforts of the Commission, and indeed the Italian government, in 1969 had little immediate impact, but did maintain the profile of the issue. After 1969, a combination of factors elevated the status of regional policy: the issue of economic and monetary union (EMU); the proposed enlargement of the Community to include the UK and Ireland; and the issue of national aids to industry.

The Treaty of Rome's objective of completing economic and monetary union was given impetus by the *Werner Report* of 1970. This report provided a plan to achieve economic and monetary union in the Community within ten years, necessitating institutional reform and closer political integration. The *Werner Report* also concluded that continued regional disparities within the Community would militate against EMU being achieved. From the subsequent agreement to work towards EMU, taken at the Hague Summit of 1969, came a recognition from the Council that some form of action would be needed to remedy the problem of regional imbalances. The prospects of further enlargement brought another dimension to the context of the introduction of EC regional policy.

The proposed enlargement of the Community to include Denmark, Ireland and the UK would bring a new set of disadvantaged regions to be dealt with in two of these countries. While the problems of Ireland, largely related to agriculture, might have been dealt with by reforming the EAGGF, the UK had a number of regions suffering industrial decline. Moreover, the UK was also likely to be a net contributor to Community funds and was subsequently keen to explore avenues through which it could secure reimbursement.

The third factor providing the context for the introduction of EC regional policy was the Commission's plans for controlling Member State aid to industry. In June 1971, the Commission recommended to the Council that state aids should be clearly measurable (transparent) and that there should be a distinction between the 'central' or wealthy areas of the Community and the 'peripheral' regions. The level of state aid to central areas should be no more than 20 per cent of total investment (H. Wallace 1977b: 142). In line with Treaty of Rome provisions to ensure fair competition within the Community, the Council endorsed this proposal in October 1971. The effect was to encourage a higher proportion of national aid to be targeted at less favoured regions. As such, the decision placed constraints on national regional policy and thus intensified interest in developments at Community level.

The Paris Summit of 1972 and its Aftermath
By 1972, regional policy was high on the Community agenda. The Commission's proposals had been accepted unanimously by the European Parliament in March 1972 and in the same month the Council of Ministers agreed to take a decision on the regional policy issue by October. At the Paris Summit of October 1972, the new Member States were involved in discussing future priorities for the first time and it became clear that senior political leaders had accepted the case for a regional policy. The final communication of the summit outlined the agreement that a 'high priority' should be given to correcting the Community's structural and regional imbalances that might affect the realization of economic and monetary union. Further, the heads of government invited the Commission to prepare a report on the Community's regional problems and suggest appropriate solutions. It was also agreed that Member States would undertake to coordinate their regional

policies and that a (European) Regional Development Fund be established. The ERDF, in coordination with national aids,

> should permit, progressively with the realization of economic and monetary union, the correction of the main regional imbalances in the enlarged Community and particularly those resulting from the preponderance of agriculture and from industrial change and structural unemployment (Vanhove and Klaassen 1987: 402).

For advocates of a significant Community role in regional policy, it appeared that the main battle had been won, but it was a difficult journey from this declaration to the formal introduction of the ERDF in 1975.

From Policy Decision to Policy Detail
In the new Commission of the enlarged Community, the UK secured the regional policy portfolio. This post was filled by the pro-European George Thomson, a former Labour government minister. Thomson quickly set about the task of producing the regional policy proposals with which the Commission had been charged. The result was the *Report on the Regional Problems in the Enlarged Community* of May 1973, which became more commonly known as the *Thomson Report*. This report provided a Community-wide analysis of regional problems, noting that the wealthiest regions remained five times more prosperous than the poorest. The report outlined the main features of an EC regional policy, set out how the ERDF would operate, and provided principles for coordinating national regional policies. This included the principle later termed *additionality*, that Community regional funds should not be a substitute for national expenditure in the regions; the principle of *coordination*, bringing together the various common policies and financial instruments that existed at Community level to improve their effectiveness in meeting regional objectives; and the principle of *concentration*, requiring that Community funds be focused on those regions most in need, according to 'objective' Community-wide criteria (including unemployment rates, depopulation rates and income levels) (Commission 1973).

   The *Thomson Report* recognized the need for a Community regional policy to be implemented in conjunction with states' own policies. At the same time, 'in rejecting the principle of "juste retour" and arguing for the allocation of resources on objective Community wide criteria of regional disparity, the Commission's objectives looked forward to a time when national policies would be less important than Community ones' (Preston 1984: 66).

On 25 July 1973, the Commission laid before the Council the draft for a decision establishing a Committee for Regional Development to work towards the coordination of national policies. This would comprise two members from each state and a representative from the Commission. At the same time, the Commission put to the Council a proposal to establish the ERDF. The ERDF would have 2250 Million Units of Account (MUA) (approximately £860 million) allocated to it for a three-year period and would be distributed on the basis of 'objective Community indicators'. There would be no national quotas, but it was proposed that only areas that had been designated for by national governments for domestic regional assistance would be eligible for Community support.

A decision on the Commission proposals was expected in the autumn of 1973, but by September the scale of the obstacles in the way of agreement had become clearer. There was conflict between Member States over both the general principles of regional policy suggested and the detailed proposals of the *Thomson Report*: 'These ranged from the enthusiasm of the *demandeurs*—Britain, Ireland and Italy—to the caution of Germany the chief paymaster, with various degrees of enthusiasm and reluctance being expressed by other governments' (H. Wallace 1977b: 145).

Halstead (1982), in his study of the negotiations, suggested that the UK, Irish and Italian governments were pushing for a larger regional fund, while the West German and Belgian governments favoured a small fund. The Irish and Italian governments also considered that the elimination of regional imbalances should be a prerequisite for EMU, whereas the Danish government argued that the achievement of EMU would contribute to the reduction in regional disparities. The French government was concerned to avoid excessive interference from the Commission in its domestic policies, while the Luxembourg government was simply anxious to receive a share of the funding.

Following the Commission's publication of the proposed eligible areas in October 1973, more disagreements emerged. In particular, the German, Dutch and Danish governments thought the eligible regions were too widely drawn (covering a third of the Community population). This argument for greater concentration was in part linked to the hope of these potential paymasters, Germany being the largest, that this might limit the size of the fund. The Irish and Italian governments, potential beneficiaries, also argued for concentration, while supporting a larger fund than the Commission originally proposed. Finally, the UK government, while favouring a larger fund, also wanted greater flexibility in geographical targeting.

It became clear from the early exchanges that intergovernmental bargaining over the size and distribution of the fund would come to dominate the creation of the ERDF. As Preston put it:

> whilst the different national positions were still capable of mutual adjustment it was becoming clearer that the major protagonists saw the Fund issue in terms of national interest. The attitude adopted on the problem of eligible regions were conceived primarily in terms of the 'politics of redistribution' rather than of the 'economics of regional development' (Preston 1984: 68).

While the national interest considerations of member governments were the overriding determinant of the outcome of the regional fund negotiations, even at this early stage the Commission had played a significant role in keeping the issue alive and putting forward proposals. However, the context of the negotiations changed significantly with the outbreak of the Yom Kippur War in October 1973.

The Copenhagen Summit of December 1973 was dominated by the OPEC boycott of oil shipments to the Dutch and the decrease in oil exports to the other eight Member States (Halstead 1982: 71). Not only did these events overshadow consideration of regional policy, they impacted directly on the positions taken by national governments. Previously, negotiations had taken place against a context of economic growth: now, the likely paymasters for a regional policy, West Germany in particular, would think again. More generally, the oil crisis made it unclear how far national governments would look to EC solutions faced with the prospect of domestic recession.

Helen Wallace (1983b: 93) argued that the oil crisis, in particular 'had the dual effect of preoccupying the immediate attention of governments and of suggesting a linkage between the two issues to the German Government'. The consequence of this linkage was that the German government reflected on its previous enthusiasm to pay for a regional policy from which there would be no immediate return. Germany became particularly antagonistic towards the claims of the potentially oil-rich UK government, which was pleading a special case for assistance from the new regional fund.

Negotiations came to a turning point when the UK government refused to give Community members preference for its oil in return for UK benefits from the regional fund. Argument over this changed the spirit in which negotiations took place: 'in failing a major test of solidarity, member states subsequently felt less inclined towards any financial or 'spiritual' generosity towards each other' (Preston 1984: 69).

As progress on the Commission's proposals gradually ground towards a halt, a new dimension was introduced into the negotiations with the election of a minority Labour government in the UK in February 1974. The new government was committed to renegotiating the UK terms of the entry to the Community and to holding a referendum on continued membership. With the UK government's interest in the proposed regional fund marginalized, the prospects for agreement on regional policy became even more distant.

Despite the UK 'problem', however, the Commission maintained its efforts on regional policy and was supported in its efforts by the Irish and Italian governments. Prospects for renewed progress on regional policy were enhanced with the elections of both Schmidt in Germany and Giscard in France in the autumn of 1974: 'for Schmidt in particular the impending British referendum on EC membership highlighted the need to bring the whole protracted debate to a speedy conclusion' (Preston 1984: 74). However, no significant progress was made until the end of 1974 when the Irish and Italian governments threatened to sabotage the Paris Summit scheduled for December that year unless other member governments gave a firm commitment to establishing a regional fund. Concerns remained primarily about the fund's distribution and the eligibility criteria. However, largely in response to Irish and Italian threats, Member States agreed at the Paris Summit to establish a regional fund for a three-year period to begin on 1 January 1975. Initially, the French government interpreted this as a trial period, but, following the angry reaction of the Irish and Italian governments, all parties accepted that the fund would be permanent but should be reviewed triennially (Preston 1984: 77-78).

Provisions of the 1975 Agreement

Once the European Parliament had authorized the creation of a supplementary budget to finance the fund, the ERDF was formally established in March 1975. The ERDF would fund up to 50 per cent of the cost of regional development projects in targeted regions. The remaining cost would be provided by domestic sources. This so-called 'match-funding' requirement would ensure that EC and national initiatives would be coordinated and complementary. In addition, the fund regulations called for close cooperation between Community and national authorities in implementing regional policy.

Projects funded through ERDF fell under two broad categories: industrial and infrastructure. Both types were concerned either directly or indirectly with job creation. Applications would be submitted by national government departments to DG XVI of the Commission, which was authorized to approve projects to be submitted for approval to the Fund Management Committee (composed of representatives of the Member States and chaired by the Commission). A Regional Policy Committee was also created, consisting of two representatives of each Member State and one from the Commission, with the Commission also providing the secretariat. The chief tasks of the new committee would be to provide a forum through which national regional policies could be coordinated and to set the overall framework for regional policy in the Community. The committee also considered applications for infrastructure aid exceeding 10 MUA (Halstead 1982: 103).

The fund was endowed with 300 MUA for its first year of operation and 500 MUA for each of the following two. This total of 1,300 MUA (approximately £500 million) fell some way short of the Commission's original proposal at the Paris Summit of 1972 for 3,000 MUA, but was welcomed as progress. At the same time, national governments insisted that the distribution of the regional fund should take place according to national quotas, failing to agree on the Commission's proposals for 'objective' criteria. Moreover, all governments insisted on a quota, even though this meant some regions in richer Member States were eligible despite having a greater per capita GDP than some ineligible regions in poorer Member States (Halstead 1982: 275).

The result of national governments pursuing national advantage was a dispersed rather than concentrated distribution of funding: the ERDF would cover some 60 per cent of the geographical area of the Community and 40 per cent of the total population (Mawson, Martins and Gibney 1985: 30). Overall, there would be three net beneficiaries of the fund—the UK, Ireland and Italy—and six net contributors. The quotas agreed are set out in Table 2.1.

Table 2.1: ERDF National Quotas (1975)

	Percentage
Belgium	1.5
Denmark	1.3
France	15.0
Germany	6.4
Italy	40.0
Ireland	6.0
Luxembourg	0.1
Netherlands	1.7
United Kingdom	28.0
	100

(Ireland was also to receive a further 6 MUA taken proportionally from the other countries, with the exception of Italy.)

Source: Preston 1984: 75.

The German government had been an important ally for the Commission in seeking precise rules for the implementation of regional policy. This was particularly the case with the principle of additionality. The intergovernmental disputes following the outbreak of the Yom Kippur War led the German government to adopt a more 'hard-headed' approach to the ERDF, 'particularly in their view that any Community expenditure on regional development should be subject to precise rules to avoid national treasuries simply swallowing Fund resources and then spending them as they saw fit' (Preston 1984: 70). The wording on additionality in the original ERDF regulations stated that 'the Fund's assistance should not lead Member States to reduce their own regional development efforts but should complement these efforts' (Commission 1975)

Securing the additionality of regional funds would have been a major step towards a genuine supranational element in EC regional policy. Given the expressed opposition of national governments to a supranational policy, effective implementation of this principle could not be assumed.

Domestic Politics and the Creation of the ERDF: The UK Position

The UK government's approach to the early ERDF negotiations has typically been described either as 'ambiguous' (Wise and Croxford

1988: 175), 'ambivalent' (H. Wallace 1977b: 151) or 'ambivalent and, to a large extent, contradictory' (Preston 1984: 73). The Wilson governments of 1964–70, 'simply sought reassurance that Community rules would not impede its freedom of manoeuvre in the allocation of economic resources to regional development' (H. Wallace 1977b: 151).

The Heath government of 1970–74 had less of a commitment to domestic regional policy to protect than its predecessor and, as more pro-European, was, 'urgently in need of actions which could be used to show a sceptical public and Parliament that concrete benefits were resulting from common market membership' (Wise and Croxford 1988: 173). As such, the Heath government's enthusiasm for a Community regional policy was evidently more instrumental than ideological: 'All that was being sought was an institutionalised subsidy from the Community for British expenditure in the regions. An integrated Community policy for regional development was not on the agenda' (George 1985: 146).

The UK position on the ERDF was driven by domestic factors. During the crucial period of the Heath government, two factors were particularly important: the possible impact of EC regional policy on domestic state aid policy; and the probability that an already suspicious UK electorate would see the development compromising the government's ability to respond to difficult economic circumstances. At the same time, however, the UK government had prioritized the creation of a regional fund as a means of both reimbursement and of demonstrating the benefits of membership to its domestic constituencies. In addition, increased public demand for greater devolution of power to Scotland and Wales within the UK increased, prompting the government to see the regional fund as a means of diverting extra resources to Scotland and Wales in particular at no extra cost to the Treasury.

Yet the Heath government did not only have to satisfy demands from outside government, but also had to deal with the competing demands of its own departments:

> The Treasury's prime concern was with the balance of payments dimension and with securing financial aid that would reduce domestic expenditure; by contrast the DTI, Scottish Office and Welsh Office looked to the RDF as a source of extra support for their client groups (H. Wallace 1977b: 153).

Almost two decades later, a dispute over the direction of ERDF receipts in the UK was to reveal remarkably similar inter-departmental conflicts over the RECHAR programme (see Chapter 5). In the 1970s at least, these disputes meant that 'the possibility of a well integrated policy was thus constrained by intra as well as intergovernmental compromise' (Preston 1984: 73).

However, the relegation of the regional fund issue at EC level, following the election of a Labour government in 1974, was accompanied by its relegation in the domestic arena. As the matter fell from public view, public expectations of EC regional policy diminished:

> This, combined with increasing inflation, strengthened the hand of the Treasury in arguing that Britain's share of RDF should not increase the total expenditure on regional development in the UK, but rather cushion it against setbacks (H. Wallace 1977b: 154).

When regional policy negotiations resumed, the Labour government was concerned to retain national government control over the process to ensure that EC regional fund receipts could be directed to areas prioritized domestically and not by the Commission. The importance of securing national government control over the implementation of EC regional policy became even greater to the UK government as the pressures for devolution for Scotland and Wales grew. With powerful assemblies in Scotland and Wales a realistic prospect, there would be potential for these subnational authorities to deal with the Commission directly over regional policy matters and bypass the national government gatekeeper. Thus, the UK government wanted to shape the outcome of EC regional policy negotiations to strengthen its domestic control. As Helen Wallace (1977b: 154) put it: 'There was a determined reluctance to allow the availability of Community funds to become a resource in domestic politics except in so far as it could be controlled by central government.'

The UK government's position in the early ERDF negotiations was therefore shaped by its domestic policy preferences: in particular, the Treasury view that ERDF should not lead to an increase in overall public expenditure in the UK. The government recognized that to act successfully as gatekeeper over the domestic financial impact of ERDF required it to act as a vigilant gatekeeper during EC-level negotiations over both guiding principles and the administrative arrangements for implementation.

The Commission's Position
As there were differences within the UK government over EC regional

policy, so were there differences within the Commission, given the linkages between regional policy and other policy areas. However, these differences were not substantive, but concerned with detail rather than broad principles. Following the Paris Summit, when the Commission became more focused on regional policy, these differences became insignificant. It was recognized that, now responsive to an enlarged Community, 'the whole Commission stood to win credit if the RDF could be set up quickly' (H. Wallace 1977b: 146).

That the eventual deal to be struck on the ERDF would be essentially the result of intergovernmental bargaining was immediately recognized by George Thomson, who consequently made no effort to construct a coalition of non-governmental interests in pursuit of his objective. Instead, '...the Commission concentrated on constructing a package of rewards that would satisfy the demandeurs and persuade the other member governments that the RDF would further their interests too' (H. Wallace 1977b: 147). The importance of regional policy to national governments was illustrated by each Member State being allocated an ERDF quota. Although in some instances the quota secured by national governments was very small, 'none was prepared to forgo the possible leverage that a stake in the Fund would give it, both in bargaining over the Regional Fund and over other policy sectors' (Preston 1984: 84).

Thus, national government representatives largely determined the nature of the original ERDF through the Council machinery. That the Commission was able to influence the agenda was important, but not decisive. This was reflected by the fact that what emerged fell some way short of a common regional policy and that control over the operation over what emerged was placed firmly in the hands of national governments.

Yet the development of a Community regional policy of any kind by 1975, when so many factors were working against it, was at least in part due to the Commission's persistence and, in particular, that of DG XVI. However, acting alone, the Commission's efforts would have been insufficient: the intervention of the Irish and Italian governments prior to the Paris Summit of 1974 was probably a decisive moment. Yet, at this early stage of regional policy, the Commission proved an important ally for those member governments favouring a substantial Community role and provided important foundations for later developments.

The Role of Subnational Government

One of the striking aspects of the emergence of the ERDF was that regional and local authorities played no part in Community-level discussions, despite being the main policy implementers. While domestic consultations with subnational authorities were a feature of coordinating national positions, national governments largely shaped the conditions for policy implementation. As such, they were thus well placed to dominate the development of regional policy with the minimum of interference from 'above' and 'below'. As Swift commented:

> The national governments decide which projects should go to Brussels, they form the committees which decide which are accepted and they are responsible for implementing the projects assisted. They present the regional development programmes and are responsible for them, and can exclude the regions from having any say on how the policy should develop (1978: 16).

While subnational authorities had been organized at European level since 1951 through the Council of European Municipalities, this body expressed support for regional policy but 'produced no detailed ideas on the specific innovations required' (Halstead 1982: 131). Its support for regional policy was largely instrumental, viewing it as a potential lever through which it might strengthen its ultimate objective of securing formal consultation for subnational authorities through a Committee of the Regions.

The Role of the European Parliament

The European Parliament was a keen supporter of the Commission's attempts to establish a regional fund. Moreover, in contrast to subnational government, the unelected Parliament was able to make a significant mark during the emergence of the fund. Following the Council decision to establish the ERDF in February 1975, the Parliament blocked the release of the necessary funds by refusing to approve the Supplementary Budget Regulation. By designating the fund's three-year endowment as 'obligatory' rather than 'non-obligatory' expenditure, the Council had effectively ruled out any significant role in the process for Parliament: only on the latter did it have effective ability to amend. So, although Parliament would be able to propose changes to the regional fund budget, any amendments would have to be supported by a qualified majority in Council, leaving national governments in firm control.

Parliament argued that the ERDF endowment should be classified 'non-obligatory' because there was no provision in the original Treaties for the ERDF and its existence was thus a discriminatory decision by the Council. Eventually, and after considerable debate, Parliament, unsure of the legal position of its argument, agreed to accept the ERDF budget proposal as it stood. However, it did not accept the principle of ERDF as obligatory expenditure. In taking this position, Parliament reserved its right to return to the issue at a future date, lest the legal position were to be clarified against it. Yet this dispute did demonstrate Parliament's keenness to exercise some control over the budgetary process and, by implication, some control over the fund's effectiveness. As with the Commission, the main impact of the Parliament's involvement at this stage was to put down a marker for greater future involvement.

Implementation Issues

Additionality
Although the Commission had accepted a limited role for itself in the initial phase of regional policy, it still hoped to exert influence over ERDF expenditure in two ways: first, through its limited discretion in approving applications; and secondly, through seeking to ensure that the funds were spent in addition to any planned domestic expenditure in Member States—the principle of 'additionality'. The Commission's effectiveness in the first of these areas would be circumscribed by national governments not substantially over-bidding and therefore restricting the Commission's discretion over the types of projects funded. As noted above, securing the additionality of regional funds would have been a major step towards a genuine supranational element in EC regional policy. This was recognized by national governments, who found convenient ways of circumventing this requirement, much to the frustration of the Commission.

The early response of governments to the principle of additionality was mixed: while the Irish and Italian governments embraced the principle, the French only did so in the first year because it coincided with domestic priorities, and made this fact clear. The German government, although initially reluctant, did embrace the principle in November

1975. The UK government's response was initially unclear because of inter-departmental tensions, mainly between the Treasury and those 'spending' ministries that expected to benefit directly from ERDF receipts. A major problem for the Commission in dealing with recalcitrant governments over additionality emerged soon after the fund's creation. This was the problem of being able to prove that regional fund receipts had not been spent additionally when national governments claimed they had. As Swift put it:

> even if the amount of total regional expenditure remains constant in the year before Community aid is received and in the first year in which it is, a government can claim that, but for Community help, their national regional expenditure would have had to be reduced by an equivalent amount (1978: 16).

If, as Halstead (1982: 123) argued, 'the principle of additionality was open to question in all member states', the UK emerged as a particular problem. In 1976, the Department of the Environment issued a circular to local authorities on the use of ERDF receipts:

> the Government would not feel able to authorise individual local authorities to undertake additional projects because of the availability of assistance from the Fund. The Government's intention is that monies received from the Fund should be passed to the authority responsible for the project and used to reduce the amount that authority might otherwise have to borrow. The unused borrowing will not be available for other schemes and the (borrowing) allocation of the authority will be abated by the amount received from the Fund (DoE 1976).

Thus, local authorities would not be able to increase their total spending on economic development projects even if in receipt of ERDF grants. In short, ERDF would not be spent additionally in the UK's targeted regions. The only possible benefit for local authorities receiving ERDF and thus the only possible 'additionality' was through savings on interest payments to councils who would not have to borrow as much money as they would otherwise. However, there was no requirement that these interest savings, a modest form of 'additionality', had to be spent on regional development—they could just as easily be used to subsidize other local authority expenditures. It was possible, however, that even this modest and non-project additionality was denied UK local authorities by a compensating reduction in the rate-support grant provided by central government (House of Lords 1982: 37).

Concerns over additionality were not limited to the ERDF. In the late

1970s, approximately 95 per cent of ESF paid to the UK went directly to the Manpower Service Commission (MSC), the government agency responsible for training provision. Evidence at the time suggested it was 'highly unlikely' that the budget of the MSC would have been smaller without the ESF contributions (Halstead 1982: 242).

The Commission's problem of getting national governments to accept additionality in principle and apply it in practice continued to be a feature of ERDF in the years that followed 1975. Subsequent reforms of regional policy were characterized by the Commission's attempts to enhance its ability to act on this.

The Involvement of Subnational Authorities
Halstead (1982: 124) noted that, while local and regional authorities were actively involved in the fund's administration in some Member States during the drafting of eligible project proposals, this was not always the case. For example, in the highly centralized French political system, with a government suspicion of Commission interference, all the important decisions were taken in Paris. Moreover, even where subnational authorities did play an active role, notably in the UK and to a lesser extent in Italy, the relevant department of national government was ultimately responsible for deciding which projects to forward to the Commission. As such, national governments remained gatekeepers between subnational and supranational contacts. This position was reinforced by the fund regulations that called for close cooperation between the Community and *national* authorities.

Conclusion

A number of factors within, below (domestic) and above (external to) the internal politics of the EC contributed to the creation of regional policy. Within the EC system, two factors were particularly important: enlargement of the Community and the political imperatives of economic and monetary union. Not only were decisions on these developments intergovernmental, but all the major decisions on the creation of regional policy were taken by the Council of Ministers; in particular at the summits in Paris in 1972 and 1974 and Copenhagen in 1973. As Preston (1984: 86) noted, 'during the negotiations proposals were consistently referred up the hierarchy of authority whenever vital national interests were claimed to be at stake'.

National governments collectively controlled the financial resources needed for establishing a regional fund and the political resources provided by the pivotal role of the Council in the Community decision-making process. In contrast, the Commission's influence was limited to the argument that its stock of technical expertise and informational resources meant it was uniquely placed to decide EC regional development priorities (Preston 1984: 88). Halstead (1982: 62) concluded that

> Despite the establishment of a Directorate General responsible specifically for regional policy matters and the statistics, surveys and memoranda produced by the Commission during the Sixties and early Seventies, no concrete advances had been made as a direct result of Commission initiatives.

This assessment seems somewhat harsh. Clearly, the Commission depended on national governments for support, but the Commission played a key role in keeping the regional policy issue alive throughout the 1960s and 1970s when many factors appeared to conspire against it. That a Community regional policy of any kind emerged by 1975 owed no small part to Commission persistence, and particularly that of DG XVI. Preston (1984: 89) argued: 'Though the Commission continually prodded the Council there was little it could do beyond reminding the Council of its Summit commitments and forging coalitions of the poorer member states within the Council's committee rooms.' In retrospect, the continual 'prodding' of the Council and 'forging of coalitions' undertaken by the Commission appears more significant than some contemporary authors thought. The Commission, and to a lesser extent the European Parliament and other allies, helped lay the foundations for more significant developments in regional policy after 1975: developments that were often the result of the Commission prodding, and forming coalitions with national governments.

The most important illustration of external events shaping the development of regional policy was the outbreak of the Yom Kippur War and the subsequent oil crisis. This event provided a jolt to assumptions about continued economic growth across all Member States. More specifically, it hardened the German negotiating position against the potentially oil-rich UK over its regional policy demands. This change in the tone of negotiations ultimately contributed to the nature of the policy that emerged. It is impossible to establish the counterfactual, but there is sufficient evidence to suggest the Yom Kippur encouraged the tendency towards a regional policy characterized by an intergovernmental 'carve-up' rather than one based on objective Community indicators.

In terms of the influence of domestic politics, a good example was provided by the different positions taken by the UK government during the period of negotiations over regional policy. The Conservative government of 1970–74 was committed to EC membership and placed a high priority on the development of EC regional policy that would illustrate to a more sceptical UK electorate the benefits of membership. The election of the Labour government, committed to negotiating the terms of entry and also to a domestic referendum on continued UK membership of the EC, brought a contrasting UK government approach to EC negotiations. Regional policy was relegated among UK government priorities and the eventual negotiating position was shaped by the political imperative of retaining national control over both the public expenditure implications and distributive impact of EC regional policy within the UK.

3 |

The Development of Regional Policy 1975–1987

Introduction

This chapter considers developments in regional policy from its introduction in 1975 to the major reform of 1988. In particular, it examines the politics and provisions of the reforms of 1979 and 1984. The conclusion reflects on the factors influencing developments and discusses early theoretical contributions to understanding the creation and early development of regional policy.

The Road to the 1988 Reform

In the period up to the major reform of the structural funds in 1988, Community regional policy underwent reforms in 1979 and 1984, the history of which was 'largely one of a struggle to throw off the many restrictions imposed by the Council of Ministers in the original 1975 Fund Regulation' (Armstrong 1989: 172). The policy package introduced in 1975, and the ERDF in particular, was subject to much criticism:

> The Fund was held to be too small and spread over too wide an area of the Community...The system of national quotas was considered too rigid and, moreover, inadequately related to the nature and seriousness of existing disparities (Mawson, Martins and Gibney 1985: 30).

Moreover, it was becoming clear that the principle of additionality continued to be interpreted as Member States saw fit. Generally, national governments viewed ERDF receipts as a form of reimbursement for their contributions to the Community budget. However, the Commission appeared powerless to change this view or the practice of denying additionality.

The 1979 Reform

In its *Guidelines for Community Regional Policy* of June 1977, the Commission stated that 'despite increased efforts by the member states and the Community to aid the development of their least favoured regions there had been no fundamental change for the better' (Halstead 1982: 135). The situation had not been helped by the oil crisis of 1973 and the subsequent weakening of EC economies which had reduced economic growth and adversely affected those regions least able to respond to the changes. The Commission argued that the continuing difficulties faced by these regions remained a serious obstacle to the effective functioning of the Common Market. In short, the need for an effective Community regional policy remained as great as ever. This required more than a simple increase in allocations. The Commission identified the need for greater flexibility in the allocation of funds, improved coordination between the ERDF and other Community policies and financial instruments and better coordination of the regional policies of Member States and increased allocations to the ERDF. In the Commission's terms, the implication of a more effective Community regional policy was a more influential role for the Commission.

In its June 1977 proposals for reform, the Commission sought to increase its influence over the distribution of ERDF by proposing that 13 per cent of funds be allocated through a non-quota section for 'specific Community measures'. These measures would target areas whose problems had been exacerbated by the direct effect of Community policies, whether these were within nationally designated assisted areas or not. For the most part, non-quota aid would concentrate on regions across Member States suffering from the decline of the same industries. The Commission was seeking to break with the rigidity of the national quota system and to 'make some modest movement towards the ERDF becoming a development agency of a more genuine "Community" character rather than a somewhat limited subsidiser of separate national policies' (Wise and Croxford 1988: 175).

Not surprisingly, the Commission's non-quota proposal met with opposition within the Council. While the Commission was strongly supported by the Dutch government, the French government rejected the proposal outright, arguing a non-quota section of spending would give the Commission too much power to interfere in what was seen as matters of domestic policy. The UK government was supportive of the French position, but kept a low profile on the issue. The German government would support the proposal only if the non-quota section was sufficiently restricted and its uses tightly defined The Irish government favoured the proposal, as did the Italian government after some initial reluctance. In addition to proposing a non-quota section, the Commission also sought to define more broadly the types of schemes that could be funded. Over both these issues, the position of national governments continued to reflect expressed national interests:

> Once again the negotiations saw the net beneficiaries, such as Britain and Italy, pushing at the reluctant Germans to broaden the scope of eligible activity, with only the smaller states, such as the Netherlands arguing for a strengthening of authority at Community level…member states were applying the criteria of national advantage applied to all Fund negotiations. This suggested that the Commission's intentions would be constrained as before (Preston 1984: 226 and 227).

The defence of national interests meant there would be little immediate change to the legal and administrative framework that had guided the operation of the fund since 1975. However, the Council eventually accepted the proposed non-quota section in June 1978, although the French government insisted this be set at a maximum of 5 per cent of ERDF. Moreover, even this limited amount was to be distributed subject to unanimous agreement in the Council, rather than by qualified majority voting as proposed by the Commission.

The national quotas established after considerable negotiation in 1975 were left largely unchanged when considered again by the European Council in December 1977, thus maintaining the political balance previously agreed. The biggest increase was awarded to France for its overseas departments, which had not been taken into account in the original calculations. The French government had made this increase a condition for its agreement to the overall package (Halstead 1982: 147). The new allocations were as shown in Table 3.1.

During the same December Council, it was agreed by the heads of government that the regional fund would be allocated 1850 MUA for 1978–80 (580 MUA for 1978, 620 for 1979 and 650 for 1980). The European Parliament was dissatisfied with these amounts and provoked another budgetary dispute with the Council, although accepting the 1978 level rather than risking no commitment at all for that year. Parliament was in a stronger position this time around, with ERDF being classified as non-obligatory expenditure from 1978, thus giving Parliament more power over the allocations to the regional fund.

Table 3.1: ERDF National Quotas Agreed December 1977 (1975 figures in brackets)

	Percentage	
Belgium	1.39	(1.5)
Denmark	1.20	(1.3)
France	16.86	(15.0)
Germany	6.00	(6.4)
Ireland	6.46	(6.0)
Italy	39.39	(40.0)
Luxembourg	0.09	(0.1)
Netherlands	1.58	(1.7)
United Kingdom	27.03	(28.0)
	100	(100)

Source: Preston 1984: 226.

The compromise that eventually emerged in March 1979 provided an allocation for that year of 945 MUA—a significant increase which signalled to the Council that Parliament should be consulted at an earlier stage in the process if it wished to avoid future budgetary conflicts. Yet this compromise did not constitute the surrender of any real authority by the Council to the Community institutions: 'the essential political bargain upon which the Regional Fund was based…remained unchanged' (Preston 1984: 233).

One important illustration of the continued Member State dominance of ERDF was the fact that the 1979 reform contained no movement on the issue of additionality. This was despite the efforts of the European Parliament, which had been lobbied to push for changes by subnational authorities in regions denied additional resources by national governments' interpretation of the principle. This significant omission and the moderate content of the other changes continued to stifle the development of a significant relationship between subnational authorities and the Commission in the regional policy sector and confirmed the gatekeeper role of national governments.

From the Commission's perspective, probably the most significant development stemming from the 1979 reform was the use it made of non-quota aid, over which it had greatest discretion. Non-quota programmes were designed primarily to develop new alternative economic activity in regions across Member States affected by the decline of a single dominant industry—steel, shipbuilding, textiles, fisheries. A programme to assist development in border areas provided the only non-sectoral variant. Here the Commission pioneered the use of the 'programme contract'—an interrelated package of initiatives drawn up in agreement with Member States, with explicit objectives to address a clearly identified regional problem. Previously, individual projects and not packages of projects had been funded. These programmes were to prove important models for the Commission in shaping its proposals for a further reform of regional policy. Moreover, the Commission's influence over the non-quota programmes and the greater visibility of the sectoral programmes provided the Commission with potentially the greatest opportunity for securing compliance with the additionality principle.

Finally, in the negotiations for 1979 reform, the Commission argued for a more integrated use of the various funds with a regional dimension—the ERDF, ESF, EAGGF (Guidance Section) and loans from the EIB and ECSC. The Commission argued that the regions targeted would benefit from 'synergy effects'; funds used together would produce results greater than the sum of improvements gained by separately funded projects carried out in isolation (Halstead 1982: 261). This argument was accepted, and the first experiments with integrated development programmes took place in Naples and Belfast. Again, the Commission stressed the importance of additionality for the success of these programmes.

Conclusion

As with the creation of the ERDF, the negotiations over the 1979 reform of regional policy were highly politicized, particularly in relation to the size and distribution of funds. Again, the key decisions were taken by national governments through the Council machinery, despite the fact that the Commission had consulted with subnational authorities and a range of other interests in drafting its proposals. For its part, the European Parliament exercised more influence than previously, in particular over the final allocations committed to the Fund. Halstead (1982: 165) argued that the Parliament's intransigence over this matter in the face of Council counter-arguments 'proved that the Parliament was determined not to be bullied by the Council of Ministers and intended to hand over to the directly-elected Parliament a meaningful platform on which to build'.

Where the Commission did exercise obvious influence over the 1979 reform package, it did so primarily over matters that did not involve finance and those that did not threaten domestic regional policies. In particular, these were matters relating to the efficiency of ERDF, such as improvements to the working of the Regional Policy and Fund Management Committee. Here, the Council had no problem with Commission proposals. In contrast, a Commission proposal that representatives of the regions should be consulted on regional policy matters was not even considered by the Council (Halstead 1982: 161). The acceptance of a non-quota section by the Council was a typical compromise between the likely beneficiary governments (of Italy and Ireland), together with the more Community-spirited and marginally affected governments (Luxembourg and the Netherlands), and those governments most strongly opposed to expanding Commission competencies (France and the UK). In this case, the Commission made progress, but in a significantly reduced form.

Overall, the changes agreed in 1979 constituted a review of regional policy rather than a significant reform. The Commission, with vital support from the European Parliament on some issues, made advances on some of its proposals but within a policy package that bore the mark of national government preferences. Due to the Parliament's intervention, the budget was larger than the Council would otherwise have agreed; and, with Parliament's support, the Commission secured Council agreement to a small non-quota section of funding. These achievements apart, regional policy would operate much as before, with 95 per cent of funding distributed on the basis of national quotas agreed at Council meetings. The additionality requirement was unchanged and consequently so were the prospects for ERDF making a major contribution to reducing regional economic disparities.

The 1984 Reform

The Initial Proposals

There were two phases to the Commission's proposals for the 1984 reform, with the initial proposals of October 1981 reworked and resubmitted in November 1983. The 1981 proposals were radical and again were based on evidence that regional disparities had persisted and widened, providing a major obstacle to the convergence of Member State economies (Halstead 1982: 199). The impact of regional policy remained limited by the restricted financial resources; insufficient concentration of resources; inflexibility in the operation of the ERDF; inadequate coordination between the Community's regional policies and national regional policies; and a lack of coordination between the ERDF and other Community policies and financial instruments.

In addition to arguing for greater allocations and for greater concentration, the Commission proposals suggested a clear definition of rules for the coordination of national regional policies across Member States; changes to the quota section in terms of both administration and geographical coverage; a significant increase in the size of non-quota allocations; and an expansion of integrated development programmes (Mawson, Martins and Gibney 1985: 38). The Commission proposed that assistance from the quota section should be distributed according to Community criteria: aid would be restricted to regions with both a per capita GDP and long-term unemployment rate of less than 75 on an index where the Community average was 100. This would require substantial change to existing national quotas, but, more importantly, it would also mean transfer of significant responsibilities for distributing ERDF away from national governments to the Commission.

The Commission also proposed that the programme contract approach, pioneered in the non-quota allocations, should gradually replace financing of individual projects for all funding. The contracts would be for three years minimum and would be agreed by the Commission and individual member governments, in close consultation with local and regional authorities and other implementing bodies. Once programme funding had been agreed, the Commission proposed passing on grants directly to the authority or agency responsible for implementation. The transition to the programme approach would take three years to complete, eventually covering all quota section applications. The Commission believed that expansion of the programme approach and payment of funds directly to the authorities concerned would improve additionality. The Commission made no proposals to address the issue of additionality more directly.

The political implications of the Commission's proposals were clear: the role of national governments would be downgraded and the programme approach would present new opportunities for the Commission to develop links with local and regional authorities at the policy implementation stage. The Commission's role would be enhanced further by a proposed increase in the non-quota section from 5 per cent to 20 per cent. In addition, the Commission proposed that decisions on which measures would be funded should be made by the Fund Management Committee and not by the existing method of a unanimous vote in the Council. Not surprisingly, this ambitious package provoked a hostile reaction from member governments and led to a period of sustained negotiations at Community level.

Almost two years after the Commission's proposals had first been announced, there was little sign of a consensus emerging between the Commission and national governments. A particular problem was the proposed reduction in national quotas to facilitate greater Commission discretion through the expansion of non-quota aid. While most Member States agreed in principle that the non-quota section should be expanded, there was no agreement on the level of increase. In part, government positions on this were determined by the figure that might maximize their total allocations under both types of assistance. The national quotas of Denmark, France, Germany and the Netherlands were under most threat from a large expansion of the non-quota section. Similarly, while all Member States agreed in principle with the Commission's proposal for greater concentration of funding on the regions most in need, all but Germany argued they should have eligible regions (Halstead 1982: 208).

Despite enthusiasm from subnational actors and some national ministries who felt they might benefit from the Commission's proposals (House of Lords 1982: xii), the stalemate that ensued prompted regional policy Commissioner Antonio Giolitti to present revised proposals to the Council.

The Revised Proposals
The revised proposals contained two main changes. The first would abolish the distinction between quota and non-quota funding and replace it with a system of 'quantitative guidelines' which would provide each Member State with a flexible ERDF allocation, constrained by upper and lower limits. This would still allow the Commission greater control over allocations but was intended to reassure Member States over the sums they would receive. The second change proposed using the programme approach for all ERDF funding, but would retain a clear distinction between 'Community programmes' and 'national programmes'.

Community programmes, to be drawn up by the Commission in consultation with Member States, would be similar to previous non-quota initiatives. Significantly, these programmes would be instigated on Commission initiative to 'directly serve Community objectives' and would as a rule 'concern the territory of more than one state'. The national programmes would be drawn up by member governments in consultation with subnational authorities and would be limited to nationally designated assisted areas. These would, however, have to be programmes of 'Community interest': that is, be consistent with Community regional development objectives. Both these and national programmes would be required to set out clearly both objectives and anticipated results.

The Council Decision
When the Council finally voted to accept the replacement of the rigid quota system, it was with the important qualification that the percentage ranges proposed would not be indicative as the Commission had wanted. Instead, the lower limit would constitute the minimum amount of ERDF resources guaranteed to Member States, conditional on sufficient satisfactory applications being made within the required time-period. The Council also set the lower limits above those proposed by the Commission, leaving only 11.37 per cent of funding to be allocated to Community programmes (see Table 3.2). Ultimately, national governments decided that quadrupling the non-quota section would leave the judgment on 'reimbursement' more in the hands of the Commission than they found acceptable.

Table 3.2: Distribution of ERDF among the States (1985)

Member State	Lower limit (%)	Upper limit (%)
Belgium	0.90	1.20
Denmark	0.51	0.67
Germany	3.76	4.81
Greece	12.35	15.74
France	11.05	14.74
Ireland	5.64	6.84
Italy	31.94	42.59
Luxembourg	0.06	0.08
Holland	1.00	1.34
United Kingdom	21.42	28.46

Source: De Witte 1986: 425.

While the Council agreed to the Commission's proposal to extend the use of the programme approach, it did so on a trial basis. Programmes would not be drawn up by the Commission as it proposed, but by 'the competent authorities of the member state or states concerned in consultation with the Commission'. Moreover, these programmes would only account for 20 per cent of ERDF by the end of the third year rather than the 40 per cent the Commission initially wanted. Here, the Commission received support from some net contributors to the ERDF, notably the German and Dutch governments. These governments were also sympathetic to Member States demonstrating additionality. In both instances, the net contributor governments were keen to ensure funds were spent effectively rather than being used by the net beneficiary governments to top up Treasury funds (Halstead 1982: 297).

In terms of total allocations to the regional fund, the 1984 reform brought an increase, but far short of that proposed by the Commission. While allocations to the ERDF had steadily increased since its creation (see Table 3.3), it remained a rather blunt instrument of regional policy 'far too small to make a significant contribution to redressing the regional imbalances within the common market' (Wise and Croxford 1988: 180).

Table 3.3: Changes in the Absolute and Relative Size of the ERDF 1975–86

Year	Size of fund	Percentage of EC budget
1975	257.6*	4.8
1976	394.3*	5.6
1977	378.5*	4.9
1978	581.0	4.6
1979	945.0	6.1
1980	1165.0	6.7
1981[†]	1540.0	7.3
1982	1759.5	7.6
1983	2010.0	7.6
1984	2140.0	7.3
1985	2289.0	7.5
1986[‡]	3176.5	9.1

*   Converted into ECU at January 1986 rate. The ECU replaced the EUA in 1979 as part of
   the European Monetary System (EMS).
[†]   Greece joins the Community.
[‡]   Spain and Portugal join the Community.

Source: Wise and Croxford 1988: 165.

Conclusion

The 1984 outcome, like that of the previous reform negotiations, turned out to be more of a review than the substantial reform the Commission intended. In particular, Community programmes that were the main supranational element under negotiation appeared to have been 'hijacked by member states' (Mawson, Martins and Gibney 1985: 56). Yet, while the increase in Commission discretion overall had been limited, the 1984 changes were viewed as a 'modest move towards the ERDF becoming an agent of regional development more influenced by Community perspectives' (Wise and Croxford 1988: 175). In particular, the introduction of minimum and maximum allocations meant the Commission had a little more discretion over grant allocations. In addition, the Commission secured agreement that a qualified majority rather than unanimity would decide Community programmes in Council. The Commission also saw the Council's acceptance of the national programme approach in modified form as a step forward. In particular, national programmes would make it more difficult 'for governments to use ERDF finance to subsidize their own efforts rather than augment them; and, by stressing the need to coordinate regional investment, the programme system would aim to tailor national policies to conform more closely with Community priorities' (Pinder 1983: 109).

The 1984 reform brought no significant movement on the issue of additionality, save for the limited changes that might develop from national programming and from increased non-quota allocations under Community programmes. The Commission hoped its increased involvement through programming would strengthen its hand on additionality. By the time of this reform, the UK government was identified as particularly difficult over the implementation of additionality. The government claimed that '[a]lthough Fund receipts for individual projects are retained by the Government, they are taken into account in determining the levels of national regional assistance which would be lower without the Fund receipts' (House of Lords 1981: 7). While this explanation appeared reasonable in terms of extra resources being provided, conflicting information from local authorities and the UK government itself (DoE 1976: Chap. 2) left the Commission unconvinced that additionality was provided. While the government appeared to have changed its position in principle from the DoE circular issued in 1976, it had not changed its implementation arrangements in practice.

There was one exception to the UK government's treatment of additionality, involving the integrated operations programme for Belfast, which proved the rule. This, according to a government official, was 'an entirely different situation'.

> Here, the Commission came along and said: 'We have this kind of money available which we are proposing to divert to the United Kingdom to finance housing in Belfast'. This was a grant which the Government could not have foreseen. Until the Commission came to offer it, we did not know it existed. Under the circumstances, and provided the money is paid in way enabling us to spend it in later years, not the year in which it is paid—because housing programmes take time—then some kind of additionality is possible (civil servant, House of Lords 1982: 5).

The inference was that additionality was only possible where EC grants could not be anticipated. Moreover, no change in the additionality wording in the 1984 ERDF regulations meant no new requirement for the UK government or others to demonstrate additionality. Moreover, it was said as early as 1985 that 'attempts to secure additionality through the identification of EC measures within RDPs (Regional Development Plans) and regional programmes can easily be overridden if member states so choose' (Mawson, Martins and Gibney 1985: 56). Thus, despite progress in some areas for the Commission, the central purpose of the funds continued to be undermined.

Conclusion

Prior to the reform of the structural funds in 1988, the consensus of opinion was that progress towards the development of a Community regional policy had 'been marred by national control over all the major aspects of the policy' (Keating and Jones 1985: 54). The struggle over regional policy was seen as

> a familiar tussle between the member governments and the Commission over whose influence should predominate: the encapsulation of crucial stages of decision in the Council of Ministers and frequently their adjudication by the European Council (H. Wallace 1983b: 96).

Helen Wallace argued that 'by no stretch of the imagination could the story of the ERDF vindicate the approach of the functionalist or neo-functionalist' (1983b: 97).

While most early accounts attached some significance to the Commission's role, and to a lesser extent that of the European Parliament, national governments were seen to dominate an EC-level process restricted largely to institutional actors. There was 'almost no scope for the direct involvement of extra-governmental interests for regional lobbies or other pressure groups, much though they have lobbied and pronounced on the various proposals tabled and important though their influence may have been at the national level' (H. Wallace 1983b: 97). At the same time, the creation and early development of regional policy suggested that the idea of a straightforward Commission–Council dialogue was too simplistic to describe the decision-making processes of the EC. As Halstead (1982: 287) argued:

> On the one hand there is the open-ended policy of the European Commission and the input from the local, regional, national and European subsidiary linkages. On the other hand this side of the scales is counterbalanced and indeed outweighed by the strength and intransigence of the member state representatives in COREPER, the Council of Ministers and the European Council. In addition the member states have exercised control over the Commission through their representation on the Fund Management and Regional Policy Committee which consider and control the decisions taken on project applications in Brussels.

In looking for an appropriate analytical framework to explain the early development of EC regional policy, Helen Wallace (1983b: 98) stressed the need to take into account two things. First, that the ERDF emerged from a controversial debate within the Community regarding resource distribution at both EC and national level, central to which was the point that 'to give EC institutions authority over regional policy is to enable influence to be exerted over allocative decisions both among and within states, territory which is contested on both political and economic grounds'. Secondly, Wallace emphasized that regional policy is a horizontal, not vertical, policy sector. As such, it has repercussions for economic and social welfare in general, for patterns of employment and for agricultural and industrial development. Not only does this limit the scope for the 'systematic mobilisation of interests', but also means that regional policy does not, 'readily permit the interactions through the formally established hierarchy of committees to acquire a life and purpose of their own in the way that has characterised agricultural policy in the EC'.

Where the Commission made progress, it did so through its agenda-setting powers. Thus, while national governments rejected and diluted many of the Commission's proposals for regional policy from the 1960s through to the early 1980s, it was significant these were Com-

mission proposals and some were adopted. The creation and development of both the non-quota system and programme contracts were
examples of this. In particular, the Commission had the expertise and
information to prepare solid arguments for these, and secured sufficient
support within the Council.

Up to the 1988 reform of the structural funds, the Commission, at
times assisted by the European Parliament, made piecemeal progress by
seeking to 'educate and cajole governments at the margins rather than
to promote immediate and radical changes in national regional policies'
(H. Wallace 1983b: 97). Yet advances for the Commission depended a
sufficient number of national governments accepting its arguments,
which in many instances did not happen. Additionality was an important example of this and the Commission's failure to make progress on
this key principle was an illustration of the Council's resilience on
matters of 'high policy' to national governments.

The consequence of national government domination was the failure
of the Commission to establish a regional fund with the redistributive
effects it desired. The reform of the structural funds in 1988 would provide another opportunity for the Commission to secure its objective. Up
to that point, however, the consensus was that 'Little has yet happened
to disprove that the Fund is essentially "cosmetic" and conceals the
lack of a genuine desire among member states to adopt interventionist
policies at a Community level capable of reducing spatial inequalities
in wealth' (Wise and Croxford 1988: 187).

However, while the reforms of 1979 and 1984 failed to convert
ERDF from a system of reimbursement to an effective instrument of
regional policy, they contained the seeds for future policy development
as seen in the 1988 reform.

4 |

The Development of Regional Policy 1988–1993

Introduction

The 1988 reform of the structural funds is widely accepted as being the most significant after the creation of regional policy in 1975. This chapter considers the politics and provisions of that reform. Negotiations over the principle of additionality are discussed in detail. Following consideration of the revisions to structural policy agreed in the 1993 reform, the chapter concludes by looking at the factors explaining developments in the whole period after 1988.

The 1988 Reform of the Structural Funds: The Context

Two important developments provided the political and economic context of the reform of the structural funds that came into effect on 1 January 1989: the enlargement of the Community to include Portugal and Spain in 1985; and the push towards greater economic and social cohesion given expression in the Single European Act (SEA) of 1986.

Enlargement

The most significant implication for regional policy of the accession of Spain and Portugal was the considerable widening of regional disparities in the EU. This enlargement led to 'a doubling of the population of the least favoured regions (those with per capita GDP of less than 50% of the Community average)' (Commission 1989: 9). This in itself required an expansion of regional policy. However, the accession of Spain and Portugal was also important in prompting the introduction of a new type of programme: the Integrated Mediterranean Programmes (IMPs).

The IMPs were introduced in response to Greek threats to veto the accession of Portugal and Spain made at the Dublin European Council in December 1984. The Greek government argued this enlargement would damage Greece economically and that compensation should be agreed for this before admitting the new members. In recognition of the Greek argument, the Brussels European Council meeting of March 1985 agreed the IMP initiative to compensate Greece, Italy and France.

Hooghe (1996a) points to the creation of the IMPs as important forerunners for the reform package of 1988. An important feature of the IMPs was that they 'advocated continuing involvement of the Commission in all aspects of programming and aimed to mobilize "non-central" actors' (Hooghe 1996a: 11). The operational arrangements for IMPs were designed by a small unit attached to the Commission, there being 'no evidence of member state influence, nor of formal consultation with other services' (Hooghe 1996b: 97). This unit was later upgraded to DG XVII and this directorate was central to drawing up the 1988 structural fund regulations.

Expansion of the EC had previously been a factor in shaping regional policy. As noted earlier, impetus for the creation of the original regional fund in 1975 owed much to the accession of the UK in particular. In the mid-1980s, however, expansion was accompanied by the most determined push for the completion of the Common Market in the Community's history. Together, these factors provided the unique context of the 1988 reform of the structural funds.

The Push for Completion of the Internal Market
The fact that the economies of the US and Japan were outpacing the bulk of Community economies in the late 1970s and 1980s initially provoked the response of greater national protectionism from some Member States—so much so that the European Economic Community was pronounced 'moribund' in 1982 (see Keohane and Hoffman 1991: 1). Soon after, however, the general focus of Member States was on the Community's need to achieve a genuine common market if the relative poor performance of EC economies was to improve. It was in this context that the newly appointed Delors Commission's White Paper of 1985 led to the SEA, which in turn resulted in almost 300 legislative proposals for enactment by the end of 1992. These proposals intended to remove by that date all existing physical, technical and fiscal barriers to the movement of goods, people and services within the Community, creating a Single European Market (SEM).

The restructuring of Member State economies necessitated by the SEM led to talk of a 'Golden Triangle' connecting the prosperous parts of the Community which would benefit most from the single market. The implication was that regions outside this triangle faced relative exclusion from the benefits in the absence of an effective Community regional policy. In short, the impetus given by the SEM 'served to alert the poorer regions of the Community that the completion of the internal market could lead to a concentration of wealth in the EC's core economies' (McAleavey 1993: 92).

In response to the concerns of the Community's poorer regions, Article 130A of the SEA set out the need to strengthen 'economic and social cohesion' within the EC, in particular by aiming at 'reducing disparities between the various regions and the backwardness of the least-favoured regions' (Commission 1989: 11). The term *cohesion* subsequently came into use to describe a range of Community policies, including structural policy, aimed at reducing regional and social disparities. It was, as Hooghe (1996b: 123) notes,

> the most political imaginative term out of a string of alternatives such as 'structural policy', 'redistribution', 'solidarity/equity mechanism', 'convergence', 'regional and social development', or even 'social dimension', which were considered by circles close to Jacques Delors during the negotiations for the Single European Act.

The concept was developed within the Commission as the counterpart of the moves to completing the internal market. It had a dual meaning:

> It summarized a novel policy rationale to deal more effectively with the old problem of regional economic disparities, but it also held a political promise to involve subnational actors more openly in European decision-making... subnational mobilization was crucial to its success (Hooghe 1996b: 89).

By formally building into it the goal of social and economic cohesion, the SEA was 'much more than a great step forward on the road to integration. It also substantially changed the *nature* of the process of integration' (Nanetti 1996: 59; emphasis original).

Article 130D of the SEA called for a reform of the three structural funds (ERDF, ESF and EAGGF), through a framework regulation on their tasks, their effectiveness 'and on co-ordination of their activities between themselves and with the operations of the EIB and other financial instruments' (Commission 1989: 11). The Commission commented that the SEA 'clearly establishes the principle, hitherto implicit in the EEC Treaty of solidarity between states…It requires not only increasing convergence of Member States economic policies but also a reduction in regional disparities' (Commission 1989: 11).

The Commission was charged with the task of presenting to the Council a comprehensive proposal on the reform of the structural funds. To facilitate this process, the Commission produced draft regulations in February 1987, which formed the basis for legislation to improve the coordination of the previously separate ERDF, ESF and EAGGF. The Brussels European Council of February 1988 agreed the draft regulations in principle and also agreed to a doubling of structural fund allocations by 1993. The final details were agreed in three main regulations that came into effect on 1 January 1989.

Provisions of the 1988 Reform

The Council agreed that allocations to the three structural funds would double in real terms between 1987 and 1993, with allocations in the final year of this period up to ECU 14 billion; approximately 25 per cent of the EU budget. This contrasted sharply with the initial allocation of ECU 257.6 million in 1975 which represented 4.8 per cent of total EC spending and the 1987 allocation of ECU 3,311 (9.1 per cent) (Marks 1992: 194). The operation of the funds would be guided by four complementary principles, which were essentially the ones the Commission had advocated throughout the development of regional policy. These were:

- *concentration* of the funds on the areas of greatest need as defined by the accompanying objectives (see below);

- *programming*: multi-annual programmes would be the norm for all funding, to ease the Commission's administrative burden and promote a more coherent approach;

- *partnership*: partnerships would be established to oversee the administration of the funds and would require the formal involvement of subnational authorities for the first time;

- *additionality*: the additionality requirement would be strengthened by a new regulation and by the greater involvement of subnational authorities and the Commission in the new partnership arrangements.

Concentration

Following the principle of concentration, structural fund expenditure was focused on five objectives: three with an explicit regional dimension (Objectives 1, 2 and 5a). The bulk of spending was focused on the most disadvantaged regions eligible under Objective 1 (approximately 65 per cent of total structural fund allocations).

Table 4.1: Priority Objectives of the 1988 Reform

Objective 1: promoting the development of 'less developed regions' (those with per capita GDP of less than, or close to, 75 per cent of the Community average under 'special circumstances') *(ERDF, ESF and EAGGF [Guidance Section])*.

Objective 2: converting the regions seriously affected by industrial decline *(ERDF, ESF)*.

Objective 3: combating long-term unemployment (assisting people aged over 25 unemployed for over a year) *(ESF)*.

Objective 4: assisting the occupational integration of young (people below the age of 25) *(ESF)*.

Objective 5: (a) accelerating the adjustment of agricultural structures *(EAGGF [Guidance Section])*; (b) promoting the development of rural areas *(EAGGF [Guidance Section], ESF, ERDF)*.

In addition to the 'mainstream' structural funds allocated according to the five objectives, approximately 9 per cent of the ERDF budget was retained for 'Community Initiatives'. These were programmes devised by the Commission to meet outstanding regional needs. As with the non-quota and Community programmes, such as RESIDER (steel areas) and RENAVAL (shipping and shipbuilding areas), Community Initiative programmes would primarily address the needs of specific types of regions, such as those suffering from the decline of a dominant industry.

The Council decided *eligibility for* assistance under Objective 1 and the designated areas were listed in the Framework Regulation. Seven Member States qualified for assistance under this objective. This included coverage for the whole of Greece, Ireland and Portugal.

Eligibility for assistance under Objective 2 was negotiated between the Commission and national governments following proposals of over 900 regions by Member States (McAleavey 1995a: 157). Ultimately, 60

Table 4.2: Indicative Allocation of Objective Funds by Member State for 1989–93

	Objective 1 (%)*	Objective 2 (%)†	Objective 5b (%)‡
Belgium		5.0	1.25
Denmark		0.8	0.88
France		17.6	36.82
France	2.1		
(overseas departments)			
Germany		8.6	20.14
Greece	16.2		
Ireland	5.4		
Italy		6.1	14.77
Italy (southern)	24.5		
Luxembourg		0.5	0.09
Netherlands		1.9	1.69
Portugal	17.5		
Spain	32.6	19.7	10.93
UK		39.7	13.43
UK (Northern Ireland)	1.7		
	100.0	100.0	100.00

Greece, Ireland and Portugal did not receive Objective 2 funding as they were eligible in their entirety under Objective 1.

* Source: Commission 1989: 18.
† Source: Commission 1990.
‡ Calculated from figures in Wishlade 1996: 35.

regions in nine Member States were eligible. The politics of designating the Objective 2 areas meant that population coverage was considerably higher than provided for in the Framework Regulation. The ceiling was set at 15 per cent of the population in the areas not eligible for Objective 1 (11.7 per cent of the total population). As Wishlade (1996: 36) noted: 'It is a measure of the controversy surrounding the objective 2 designation that coverage reached some 16.7 per cent of the total Community population'.

Objective 5b involved relatively small amounts of funding (ECU 2.6 billion), equal to 7 per cent of the Objective 1 allocation. As such, deciding eligibility was less controversial and covered 5 per cent of the Community population spread across nine Member States (Greece, Ireland and Portugal being the exceptions).

Together with allocations from the non-regional Objectives 3, 4 and 5a, the share of structural funding received by each Member State is detailed in Table 4.3.

Table 4.3: Total Allocation of Structural Funds by Member State 1989–93*

	Percentage
Belgium	1.18
Denmark	0.64
Germany	9.56
France	9.38
Greece	11.96
Ireland	7.08
Italy	17.08
Luxembourg	0.09
Netherlands	1.15
Portugal	13.42
Spain	20.81
United Kingdom	7.65
	100.00

* Excluding Community Initiatives

Calculated from figures in Commission 1996a: 145.

Despite the creation of new objectives with detailed criteria for eligibility, the decisions on which regions (and thus Member States) received assistance under both Objectives 1 and 2 were either taken or heavily influenced by national governments. Yet, as McAleavey (1995a: 159) put it: 'Even if an element of the "carve-up" approach did remain, the advances made by the European Commission on the other key principles were more radical.'

Programming
After more than a decade of trying, the Commission finally secured Council support for multi-annual programmes for all structural funding. This switch promised greater coherence in formulating strategies for regional development and brought a certainty to funding that had previously been absent. Objective 1 regions received programme funding for five years and Objective 2 regions for three. The shorter time-period for Objective 2 programmes was to allow flexibility for structural funds to respond to regional problems caused by unforeseen industrial decline.

Programmes would be developed through a three-stage process. First, after full consultation with the subnational implementers, national governments would submit development plans to the Commission. Each of these would provide details of the region; set out a development strategy; indicate priorities; and estimate the funding needed. Secondly, the Commission would incorporate national views in Community Support Frameworks (CSFs). These would prioritize spending areas, outline the forms of assistance and provide a financial plan. Thirdly, detailed operational programmes would be agreed by the partners, identifying appropriate measures, beneficiaries and costings to allow partners to implement the objectives of the CSFs. Beyond this, each programme would be monitored and assessed to ascertain whether money had been spent appropriately (Commission 1989).

Partnership

The principle of partnership has formed part of the Commission's view of regional policy since the 1970s. McAleavey draws attention to the *First Annual Report on the European Regional Development Fund* (1976) which stated that 'Community regional policy is by its nature a partnership between the Community and its Member states, and with the former at the present stage the junior partner' (1995a: 167). Subsequent Commission attempts to involve subnational authorities in consultations for structural policy-making had received a mixed response. In the UK, for example, the 1984 reform agreement to consult subnational authorities had little impact, with the government 'reluctant to allow local authorities much say in the preparation of the non-quota programmes' (Mawson, Martins and Gibney 1985: 49). Such consultation was made a formal requirement by the 1988 reform through the adoption of the partnership principle.

The Framework Regulation adopted by the Council in 1988 formally defined partnership as:

> close consultation between the Commission, the member states concerned and the competent authorities designated by the latter at national, regional, local or other level, with each party acting as a partner in pursuit of a common goal (Regulation [EEC] 2052/88).

Partnerships were to be active in the management, presentation, financing, monitoring and assessment of structural fund operations, including: preparation of regional development plans for submission to the Commission; negotiation of the CSFs; implementation of the Operational Programmes; and monitoring and assessment of measures taken (Bache, George and Rhodes 1996: 303).

The partnership principle was an attempt to make regional policy more effective by formally involving the subnational actors most familiar with the problems and priorities of targeted regions. Before 1988 the involvement of subnational actors had varied considerably across Member States: 'Within very broad EU guidelines, the member state was free to choose policy priorities and implement them' (Hooghe 1996b: 102). The partnership principle meant EC regional policy, for the first time, would be a policy not just *for* the regions, but also *by* the regions (Nanetti 1996: 64). Importantly, for the Commission, partnership was 'one of the more concrete examples of how the principle of subsidiarity can be put effectively into practice' (Commissioner Bruce Millan, quoted in McAleavey 1995a: 168). For these reasons, partnership was the crucial innovation of the 1988 reform.

Additionality

For the Commission, the 1988 reform provided a major opportunity to strengthen its position for securing additionality. The final wording on additionality agreed by the Council stated:

> In establishing and implementing the Community Support Frameworks the Commission and the member states shall ensure that the increase in the appropriations for the [structural] funds...has a genuine additional impact in the regions concerned and results in at least an equivalent increase in the total volume of official or similar [Community and national] structural aid in the member states concerned, taking into account the macro-economic circumstances (Article 9, Regulation 253/88 EEC).

Again, the more widespread use of programming was viewed by the Commission as a positive step toward securing additionality. From 1989, each CSF document included the following reference to the additionality regulation in Article 9:

> By agreeing to this Community Support Framework, the Member State also confirms its commitment to this legal obligation. The Commission will check the application of this commitment on a regular basis by undertaking a periodic assessment of additionality throughout the period of implementation of the Community Support Framework (Community Support Framework for Northern Ireland, 1989–93, cited in NIERC 1992: 62).

While the reform provisions on additionality appeared to enhance the Commission's prospects of ensuring effective implementation, the issue provided one of the major obstacles in the negotiations and the UK government was centrally involved (see below).

Environmental Protection

The 1988 ERDF Framework Regulation reflected increased awareness of the potential environmental threat posed by economic development operations. The regulation stated that

> Measures financed by the Structural Funds receiving assistance from the EIB or from another existing financial instrument shall be in keeping with the provisions of the Treaties with the instruments adopted pursuant thereto and with Community policies, including those concerning… environmental protection (*Official Journal of the European Communities* 1988a).

The Community Support Frameworks for Objective 1 regions also included a requirement that measures should satisfy Community legislation on the environment and that Member States should supply appropriate information to allow the Commission to evaluate the environmental impact of measures funded (Scott 1995: 81).

Negotiations over the 1988 Reform

While a number of Member States sought to limit the increase in the fund allocations, agreed in principle in the SEA, the fact that the fund was ultimately doubled owed much to the commitment of larger Member States to the single market programme. Although the funds would continue to benefit regions in the more prosperous Member States, the main impact of the doubling of the funds would be to transfer resources from Belgium, Denmark, Germany, France and the Netherlands to Greece, Spain, Ireland, Italy and Portugal with the impact on the UK largely neutral (Marks 1992: 194).

In his examination of the 1988 negotiations, Pollack (1995) suggested agreement to a substantial major reform could be explained by changes in the preferences of the various Member States—in particular the net contributors—and as a result of the accession of Greece, Spain and Portugal. The preferences of the net contributors changed in three ways. First, with the Iberian enlargement the proportion of structural funds received by the 'big three' Member States decreased significantly. This meant that, for these governments,

> the idea of greater Commission oversight seemed less like an intrusion into the internal affairs of one's own state, where EC spending was minimal, and more like a necessary oversight of the poor member states where the bulk of EC money was being spent (Pollack 1995: 372).

Secondly, the Iberian enlargement made France, like the UK and Germany, a net contributor to the EC budget, thus giving the 'big three' governments a common interest in the efficient use of the structural funds. Thirdly, the spiralling costs of both the CAP and the structural funds made the level and efficiency of EC spending a 'political issue' of increasing concern to the governments of France, Germany and the UK in the 1980s (Pollack 1995: 372).

Despite the changing preferences of national governments, which meant the larger states were less concerned about Commission 'intrusion', there were issues on which some national governments were not prepared to concede ground. This was illustrated by the position taken by the UK government on the issue of additionality.

*Additionality: A Very British Coup?**
The UK government was opposed to several aspects of the proposed reform of the structural funds, including the proposed doubling of allocations. However, it was the UK government's position on additionality that posed the greatest threat to negotiations. Negotiations over additionality began in September 1988. In December 1988, the UK government 'blocked agreement on the whole package because of additionality' (Commission official, 1995). The Commission suggested that the UK had a unique dual strategy for limiting the impact in the UK of a strengthened additionality requirement:

> During the negotiations the UK government saw the way additionality was going and as an 'insurance policy' did two things. One was to dilute the wording in the regulation so that it referred to additionality for 'increases in the appropriations of the structural funds'. The other was to ensure that the UK did not appear to benefit from such increases in the appropriations by maximising their structural fund receipts in 1988. So in parallel with pushing for changes to the wording the government submitted programmes in 1987–88 which amounted to a very large sum of money (Commission official, 1995).

At the end of 1987 and the beginning of 1988, the government submitted large programme bids for the steel areas of Yorkshire and Humberside, South Wales and Strathclyde. Other major programmes submitted were for the Mersey Basin and Birmingham. It was suggested that

---

* References to Commission and other officials cited in this section are taken from Bache 1996.

The financial allocation that these programmes represented bore no relationship to the needs of the region or per head of population. The Strathclyde programme, for example, was worth ECU 350m. It was the biggest
programme ever submitted and out of proportion to the needs of the
region. It was simply part of a strategy to maximise the receipts from the
Commission for 1988 (Commission official, 1995).

The intention of this strategy was to ensure that the UK would
receive large amounts of structural fund money in 1988, thus ensuring
that receipts for the following year would be lower. This would allow
the government to claim that as it did not benefit from the 'increase in
the appropriations' resulting from the doubling of the funds it would
not have to change its arrangements to prove additionality. For its part,
the government did not deny its role in ensuring the phrase 'increase in
the appropriations' was inserted into the regulation: 'We had that put
in. We felt we would get less after the reform and therefore we would
be able to get round Article 9' (DoE official, 1995).

While the UK government was not alone in 'peaking' its structural
fund receipts in 1988, a Commission official suggested that

no other member state did this to the same extent. The timing was
crucial because the day after such approvals are made a payment is made
from the Commission to the member state equal to half of the first year's
balance. Being aware of this, the government put a lot of the spending
commitments for the programmes into the first year (Commission official, 1995).

While other Member States had reservations about additionality, only
the UK held out on the principle after it had agreed to everything else.
Ultimately, the government agreed to the new regulation with the inser-
tion of the clause 'increase in the appropriations' when it became clear
that the Commission would approve the programmes it had submitted:
'In the end it became a numbers game. After the programmes had been
approved the government knew it wouldn't have to do anything new.
One MECU of difference would have required them to show additionality' (Commission official, 1995).

For the government, the objective was clearly to get what it considered to be the best deal possible from the reform of the structural funds
without jeopardizing the single market programme: 'At the end of the
day we had to do a deal. It was a bit of horse-trading. That is how the
Community works' (DTI official, 1995).

Within UK government, there was a feeling that the UK was being victimized by the Commission over the additionality issue. It was suggested that the Commissioner for Regional Policy had a domestic UK agenda: 'In 1988 we had this massive Article 9. I saw it as the end of the road. The ex-socialist minister was getting tough…Mr Millan was making political capital…He was using his position to influence domestic policies' (DoE official, 1995).

While the importance of this argument is difficult to assess, the Commission acknowledged that the additionality requirement coincided more with the policies of other national governments:

> Other member states were carrying out their own regional policies and additionality coincided more with their efforts. There were no problems, for example, with Greece and Portugal. There had been problems with Italy. This was essentially the result of internal North–South conflict. The bulk of structural fund money for Italy went to the South and some people in the government were against that. But only in the UK did additionality clearly conflict with national policies (Commission official, 1995).

The 1988 Reform: Conclusion

As Hooghe (1996b: 100) argued, 'the European Commission approached the reform with a distinctly political strategy designed to realize the maximum number of its preferences, and by insulating the drafting process to minimize the impact of state preferences'. However, in terms of the budgetary envelope agreed in 1988, a relatively straightforward intergovernmentalist interpretation explains the agreement. The more prosperous Member States strongly supported the completion of the single market and wanted this market extending to include Spain and Portugal. In this context, the doubling of the structural funds was accepted by the likely paymaster governments as the trade-off for securing general agreement on issues of greater importance. As Moravcsik put it:

> One provision essential to the passage of the internal market programme was the expansion of structural funds aimed at poorer regions of the EC. This provision, referred to as the 'convergence policy' was not a vital element of economic liberalization, as the Commission at times claimed, but was instead a side-payment to Ireland and the Southern nations in exchange for their political support (1991: 62).

Advocates of multi-level governance did not contest this interpretation. Hooghe acknowledged that 'state executive preferences and intergovernmental bargaining can adequately explain the initiation and evolution of the budgetary envelope, with the Commission as an observant agent' (Hooghe 1996b: 100). Marks (1992: 198) conceptualized the side-payment argument as an illustration of *forced spillover*, 'in which the prospect of a breakthrough in one arena created intense pressure for innovation in others'.

However, explanations of other aspects of the reform were less convergent. Hooghe argued that the Commission emerged 'as the pivotal actor in designing the regulations' through its 'monopoly of initiative on the institutional design' (Hooghe 1996b: 100). A good example was the inclusion of the partnership principle in the regulations, which was the major innovation of the 1988 reform:

> The insular drafting, the backing of Jacques Delors, the timing, and the careful selection of the negotiation team suggest that the Commission had not been acting on behalf of the states, but wanted to 'take them by surprise', and that it was not advancing partnership merely to solve the problem of value of money but had its own agenda. The initial reactions of the states were either negative or indicated surprise (Hooghe 1996b: 99).

Hooghe (1996b: 99) noted a shift in the Commission's priorities in the mid-1980s away from maximizing financial and legal control towards an emphasis on the policy process. While Pollack suggested that this shift was a response to national government pressure to secure 'value for money' in the funds' administration, Hooghe argued that IMPs had been more important by providing a policy model involving the mobilization of 'non-central actors':

> these regulations originated from inside the Commission, were drafted quickly, and were not sounded out in advance with national actors. They drew heavily from French territorial planning ideas and new regional development economics, as well as from learning experiences in pockets of the three funds, but there is no proof of state pressure from France or other countries (Hooghe 1996b: 99).

Partnership, therefore, was not a national government agenda, but one consistent with previous Commission attempts to increase the involvement of subnational actors in structural policy-making.

Yet the context for Commission progress on partnership and other aspects of the reform was set by national governments through intergovernmental bargains over the single market programme and enlargement. These deals meant Commission proposals were more readily accepted by national governments than previously. As Hooghe (1996b: 117) put it, the Commission's policy of cohesion which informed the 1988 reform 'was conceptualized in a period of economic optimism, Euro-institutional dynamism, a pause in the fiscal crisis of the State, and a softening of the free-market philosophy. This conjunction of circumstances may well have been unique.' So, coming at a high point of EC economic integration, the negotiations over the reform of the structural funds in 1988 allowed the Commission to advance its objective of an effective supranational regional policy. However, securing changes in the regulations was one thing; effective implementation could not be taken from granted. In particular, changes to the regulations affecting additionality had again been diluted and only then accepted reluctantly by the UK government. Whether these changes would affect the UK's approach to implementing the principle remained to be seen (see Chapter 5).

The 1993 Reform of the Structural Funds: The Context

The general thrust of the 1993 reform was one of continuity rather than radical change, with the principles and structures of the 1988 reform remaining largely intact. Yet, if the 1988 reform of the structural funds suggested the Commission had advanced its regional policy objectives, the detail of the 1993 reform suggested this advance had been halted and the Commission was facing retreat. The political and economic context in which the 1993 reform took place was very different to that of 1988 and so, consequently, was the scope for advancing Commission preferences.

While enlargement again formed part of the context, negotiations to include Austria, Finland and Sweden were relatively straightforward. The new members were relatively prosperous and posed no major sectoral impacts on other Member States (Wishlade 1996: 57). In terms of regional policy, this enlargement involved three concessions: part of Austria gained Objective 1 status; Objective 6 status for sparsely populated areas was created; and EC competition rules were adapted to accommodate the subsidy practices of the Nordic states (Wishlade 1996: 57). However, the crucial factor in shaping the context of the 1993 reform was the signing of the Treaty on European Union at Maastricht in December 1991.

The Maastricht Treaty upgraded the importance of EC regional policy in the context of further moves towards closer economic and political union. Yet the period between the Maastricht European Council and the 1993 reform of the structural funds was marked by a change in the political and economic climate. In particular, 'growing unemployment and other economic difficulties within some northern member states heightened concerns about the costs and the cost-effectiveness of Community policies' (Wishlade 1996: 48). Subsequent problems involved in ratifying the Treaty prompted concern over the progress and timetable for economic and monetary union:

> From a political perspective, the ratification of the Maastricht Treaty has highlighted some fundamental doubts among politicians and their constituents in several member states about the speed and extent of European union. The competencies of the European Commission have come under scrutiny and the concept of 'subsidiarity' has been frequently invoked to enhance the role of member states in the design and implementation of Community measures (Bachtler and Michie 1994: 789).

By the Edinburgh Summit of December 1992, 'agreement on the future Community budget (providing funding for the commitments entered into at Maastricht) was the most critical item requiring decision' (Bachtler and Michie 1994: 790). The compromise that was reached included an increase in the structural funds budget to ECU 27.4 billion by 1999, virtually doubling the amount previously allocated. The context of monetary union was crucial in securing this increase.

Following the budgetary envelope agreed at Edinburgh, the Commission's proposals for the 1993 reform were framed within the principles of concentration, partnership, programming and additionality set out in the 1988 reform. The main proposals related to eligibility criteria, programming periods and administrative arrangements. Again, Member States had different concerns. While the Irish government threatened to veto the agreement unless its share of Objective 1 funding was maintained at 13.5 per cent, several Member States wanted the right to designate Objective 2 and 5b regions themselves. For its part, the UK government objected to the new Objective 4 (see below). When agreement was reached by the European Council in July 1993, following the intervention of Commission president Delors, 'secrecy surrounded the final compromise figures...and uncertainty remained as to whether the promised allocations matched or exceeded the sums agreed at Edinburgh' (Bachtler and Michie 1994: 790).

Provisions of the 1993 Reform

Official Commission documentation suggested that, in the 1993 reform, 'the major principles adopted in 1988: concentration of effort, partnership, programming and additionality, are maintained or strengthened' (Commission 1993b: 7). Yet the evidence suggested the changes made to the four guiding principles were in some cases driven by the preferences of national governments.

Concentration
The principle of concentration continued attempts to focus aid on the areas of greatest need. To do this, some amendments were made to the existing priority objectives. While Objectives 1 and 2 were not changed in 1993, Objectives 3 and 4 were merged to create a new Objective 3. This aimed at 'facilitating the integration...of those threatened with exclusion from the labour market' (Commission 1993b: 11). The new Objective 4 was designed to give effect to new tasks laid down in the Maastricht Treaty to 'facilitate workers' adaption to industrial changes and to changes in production systems' (Commission 1993b: 11). Objective 5a maintained its initial goal of accelerating the adjustment of agricultural structures as part of the CAP reform, but a new fund was added to assist the fisheries sector: the Financial Instrument of Fisheries Guidance (FIFG). Problems arising from the decline in fishing and fish-processing activities would also be addressed through Objectives 1, 2 and 5b. Objective 5b changed slightly from the 'development of rural areas' to the 'development and structural adjustment of rural areas' (Commission 1993b: 11). Objective 6 status (see above) was added to the list.

A number of regions were given eligibility under Objective 1 for the first time in 1993, including the five new German *Länder*. Merseyside and the Highlands and Islands (UK), Hainut (Belgium), parts of Nord-Pas de Calais (France) and Flevoland (Netherlands) were included as Objective 1 regions, even though their GDP per capita was higher than the 75 per cent of the Community average originally designated. This broadened the coverage of Objective 1 funding to 26.6 per cent of the Community population, accounting for 68 per cent of all structural funding (Commission 1996a: 145).

In response to the areas submitted by Member States, eligibility for Objective 2 and 5b funds was broadened to cover 6.8 per cent (Objective 2) and 8.2 per cent (5b) of the Community population (Bachtler

The Politics of EU Regional Policy

Table 4.4: Priority Objectives of the 1993 Reform

Objective 1: promoting the development of 'less developed regions' *(ERDF, ESF and EAGGF [Guidance Section])*.

Objective 2: converting the regions seriously affected by industrial decline *(ERDF, ESF)*.

Objective 3: combating long-term unemployment and promoting entry into the labour market *(ESF)*.

Objective 4: facilitating the adaptation of workers to industrial change *(ESF)*.

Objective 5: (a) accelerating the adjustment of agricultural and fisheries structures *(EAGGF [Guidance Section], FIFG)*; (b) promoting rural development and structural adjustment *(EAGGF [Guidance Section], ESF, ERDF)*.

Objective 6: developing sparsely populated Nordic areas *(ERDF, ESF EAGGF [Guidance Section])*.

---

and Michie 1994: 791). Objective 2 regions received 11.1 per cent of all structural fund allocations (Commission 1996a: 145).

Table 4.5: Allocation of Objective 1 and 2 Funds by Member State 1994–99 (allocations for 1989–93 in brackets)*

	Objective 1 (%)		*Objective 2 (%)*		*Objective 5b (%)*	
Austria	0.17	(0.00)	0.17	(0.00)	5.87	(0.00)
Belgium	0.78	0.00)	2.22	(4.47)	1.12	(1.48)
Denmark			0.78	(0.41)	0.79	(0.94)
Finland			1.17	(0.00)	2.77	(0.00)
France	2.33	(2.18)	24.55	(19.98)	33.60	(39.16)
Germany	14.51	(6.84)	10.2	(9.48)	17.89	(22.89)
Greece	14.87	(17.18)				
Ireland	5.98	(10.18)				
Italy	15.81	(19.41)	9.52	(6.31)	13.13	(16.13)
Luxembourg			0.11	(0.19	0.90	(0.13)
Netherlands	0.16	(0.0)	4.33	(1.01)	2.19	(1.48)
Portugal	14.87	(19.28)				
Spain	27.98	(23.21)	15.73	(24.57)	9.70	(11.87)
Sweden			1.02	(0.00)	1.97	(0.0)
United Kingdom	2.51	(1.81)	29.83	(32.87)	1.97	(5.91)
Total	100.00		100.00		100.00	

*Actual allocations for 1989–93 differed slightly from the indicative allocations outlined by the Commission (1989) above. Source: Calculated from figures in Commission 1996a: 145. Excluding Community Initiatives.

Community Initiatives, which had been criticized by Member States for adding to bureaucracy, were limited by Council to 9 per cent of the total structural fund budget instead of being raised to 15 per cent as proposed by the Commission. The creation of a management committee to oversee Community Initiatives, with Member State representatives, would curtail Commission discretion over the nature, allocations and timing of these programmes.

Table 4.6: Total allocation of the Structural Funds by Member State 1994–99 (allocations for 1989–93 in brackets)*

	%
Austria	1.04 (0.0)
Belgium	1.31 (1.18)
Denmark	0.54 (0.64)
Finland	1.09 (0.0)
France	9.65 (9.38)
Germany	14.12 (9.56)
Greece	10.12 (11.96)
Ireland	4.07 (7.08)
Italy	14.29 (17.08)
Luxembourg	0.06 (0.09)
Netherlands	1.59 (1.15)
Portugal	10.12 (13.42)
Spain	22.91 (20.81)
Sweden	0.85 (0.0)
United Kingdom	8.26 (7.65)
Total	100.00

Calculated from figures in Commission 1996a: 145.
*Excluding Community Initiatives.

Programming
The revised regulations laid down a new six-year programming period to replace the previous five-year term. This was so that the end of the funding period would coincide with that of the 'financial perspectives' approach to the general EU budget decided at the Edinburgh Summit. While the CSFs for Objectives 1, 3 and 5b would be adopted for six years, two three-year phases were specified for Objective 2 with the possibility of adjusting the eligible areas and CSFs at the end of the first phase. A similar arrangement was proposed for Objective 4 CSFs.

The previous three-stage decision-making procedure for allocating funds was streamlined to two stages. Henceforth, Member States would be required to submit a single programming document (SPD) compris-

Some of the principles guiding the structural funds did not apply to the operation of the Cohesion Fund. The fund was to finance projects instead of programmes, and only those concerned with environmental or transport infrastructure, rather than a range of measures. Most importantly, however, the requirements of partnership and additionality appeared to be relaxed if not abandoned. As Scott (1995: 39) noted: 'In the first instance, nowhere in the interim instrument or in the European Council guidelines regarding the main elements of the forthcoming Cohesion Fund Regulation is there any reference to the concept of partnership.' Instead, decisions on projects to be funded would be made by the Commission in agreement with the 'Member State' concerned. In terms of additionality, the preamble to the interim regulation stipulated that Member States should not 'decrease their investment efforts in the field of environmental protection and transport infrastructure', but the more tightly defined principle of additionality included in the structural fund regulations did not apply.

While the relaxed requirements on additionality and partnership left the implementation of these principles to the discretion of Member States, this was to some degree understandable in the context of the purpose of the Cohesion Fund. The fund was designed to assist poorer Member States to meet the convergence criteria for EMU outlined in the Maastricht Treaty which required Member States to limit public borrowing to no more than of 3 per cent of GDP and their debt to GDP ratio at below 60 per cent. This implied severe constraints on public expenditure, particularly for the poorer Member States. Given this 'higher' objective, national governments were left with considerable discretion over how Cohesion Fund allocations would be spent. In particular, insistence on additionality would have created serious tension with the objective of reducing public expenditure in the 'Cohesion Four' countries.

Conclusion

While the context of the 1988 reform gave the Commission considerable scope for advancing its policy preferences, the 1993 reform represented a reassertion of national government control in key areas. A good example was additionality. The tenacity with which the Commission had sought the implementation of additionality after 1988 (see next chapter) was met by national governments effectively diluting the requirement in 1993. After 1993, the additionality requirement would take into account 'the macro-economic circumstances in which the funding takes place, as well as a number of specific economic circumstances', seemingly offering governments a number of 'opt-out' clauses. Indeed, in the context of the convergence criteria for monetary union agreed at Maastricht, for the Commission to pursue genuine additionality at this time would have been difficult: while additionality required Member States to demonstrate additional public expenditure, the convergence criteria put a squeeze on domestic public spending.

Other changes reflected the reassertion of national government preferences. For example, while the partnership principle was confirmed, national government remained in control of the designation of 'appropriate partners'. In addition, a new clause stated that the choice of partners should be consistent with 'the framework of each Member State's national rules and current practices'. This meant that where the Member State took a narrow definition of the relevant partners, this would be acceptable if consistent with national rules and current practices. This appeared to undermine the immediate prospects of the Commission satisfying its objective of ending the exclusion of certain partners. For the UK government, this meant its policy of excluding trade unions from structural fund partnership arrangements could continue without the degree of criticism from the Commission that had been a feature of the period 1988–93. Following the 1993 reform, a *Community Economic Development* priority was included in some structural fund programmes that promised to broaden the range of partners to include local community representatives. The impact of this is discussed in the following chapter.

The creation of the Cohesion Fund was a direct response to the demands of the governments of poorer Member States and provided little scope in its administrative arrangements for the innovations of structural policy. Finally, the creation of the management committee to oversee Community Initiatives (CIs) created a degree of national government involvement that would curtail Commission discretion. In the conflict over the implementation of additionality after 1988, the Commission had used its control over the content, coverage and timing of CIs to undermine UK government arguments (see next chapter). The 1993 changes meant this would be less possible in future.

In summary, the 1993 reform provided a measure of how the relative influence of actors at EU level can fluctuate within a policy sector over a short period of time. The context of regional policy reform changed dramatically in the five years after the 1988. This led to a shift in the balance of political resources away from the Commission to the Council at the EU level, which was reflected in the 1993 outcome. If the 1988 reform was characterized as a 'great leap forward' for the Commission, the 1993 reform meant several paces backwards. The extent to which policy implementation reflected Commission or national government preferences throughout the period from the 1988 reform onwards is the subject of the next chapter. An assessment of contemporary explanations of the 1988 and 1993 reforms is developed in the concluding chapter.

5 |

The Politics of Implementation
1988–1998

Introduction

As noted in the previous chapter, the framework of implementation provided by the regulations for the period after 1988 was relatively consistent. The 1988 reform set the guiding principles and these were only modified, rather than reformed, in 1993. This chapter considers the implementation of the structural funds between 1988 and 1998 (highlighting where changes in 1993 impacted on implementation). The main focus is on two key principles of the 1988 reform: partnership and additionality. Partnership, an ambitious attempt to bring together policy-makers from different levels of governance, was the crucial innovation of the 1988 reform. Additionality had been a central principle of regional policy since 1975. The 1988 regulations, however, provided the clearest statement to date of the obligation this principle placed on Member States.

Partnership

The partnership principle introduced in 1988 sought to involve the Commission, national governments and subnational authorities in the process of structural policy-making across Member States, posing a challenge to existing national practices. As Hooghe (1996a: 2) argued, this was 'a very ambitions goal, given that these uniform procedures were expected to work equally well in twelve different political systems, having diverse territorial relations and regional policy traditions, in some cases with extremely weak subnational authorities'. As such, the 1988 reform was unique in attempting to secure convergence of policy-making practices across divergent national contexts. In short, the partnership arrangements were designed 'to enable European institutions to penetrate the politics and society of the individual member state' (Hooghe 1996a: 5).

Hooghe (1996a) coordinated the most comprehensive study to date of the impact of the partnership arrangements across Member States. This study considered the impact of the partnership arrangements on 'territorial restructuring' within eight Member States. It sought to answer two related questions:

> Have diverse territorial relations converged under pressure of this uni-
> form EU policy, hence moving towards a systematic involvement of
> subnational authorities in all member states? Or are uniform European
> regulations being bent and stretched so as to uphold existing differences
> in member states? (Hooghe 1996a: 2).

The following section brings together some of the contributions to that study with other work which illustrates that, despite the 'uniform' rules, there were great differences in the way the partnership principle was implemented across Member States. It begins with a five-nation study of implementation in Objective 1 regions and is followed by looking at implementation in two of the largest Member States—Germany and the UK—with very different administrative traditions. This section concludes by looking at a recent departure in partnerships contained in the Community Economic Development (CED) priority of structural fund programmes in the UK after 1994.

Partnership in Greece, Ireland, Italy, Portugal and Spain
Nanetti (1996) looked at the participation of national, supranational and subnational actors in the implementation of the Community Support Frameworks (CSFs) in five of the seven Member States with Objective 1 regions after the 1988 reform: Greece, Ireland, Italy, Portugal and Spain. Of the five countries studied, two had regional systems (Spain and Italy); two had recently created regional administrative planning districts (Greece and Portugal), while the whole of Ireland was the territorial basis for the 'regional' plan. In assessing the role played by regional actors in the implementation process, there was a clear division 'between the decentralized and the non-decentralized countries, in terms of both how the process of implementation of the CSFs was shaped as well as the kind of outputs which were produced' (Nanetti 1996: 75).

In terms of preparing and negotiating CSFs, regions in the five Member States were at best only 'partially involved' and in the three smaller countries—Ireland, Greece and Portugal—did not participate at all. However, the process had the impact of contributing to a debate on regionalization in the smaller countries, notably in Portugal, 'where politically-charged discussions ran through the phase of CSF negotiations on the issue of regionalization, promoted by Brussels and strongly resisted by Lisbon, which did not want regional management programmes or regional administrations to manage them' (Nanetti 1996: 82). Moreover, it was in the CSF negotiating phase that partnership was defined in different national contexts. In particular, there was a marked difference in Italy and Spain from the other countries:

> In the former, it is constructed on the regional role, notwithstanding the contributions made by the respective national governments. This is very different from the interpretation given to the same concept by, for example, Portugal, where the concept of partnership was endorsed and the idea that it should be region-based rejected (Nanetti 1996: 82).

On other aspects of implementation, however, partnership was more significant. For example, regions played a more important role as *translators* of operation programmes, questioning the eligibility criteria attached to programmes and arguing for greater flexibility. Specifically in relation to the financial management of operational programmes, regions had greater autonomy than the regional planning districts. Thus, in Greece, 'those decisions were centralized at the ministerial level, just as the implementation was centralized' and in Ireland, the Department of Finance had 'overall responsibility' (Nanetti 1996: 83). In contrast, decentralized financial management went 'hand in hand with regional governance' in Italy and Spain.

Overall, the picture of CSF implementation in the first phase was 'mixed', with regional institutions in Italy and Spain having the greatest influence over development through their CSFs:

> There, planning for CSF was a three-tier process involving the Community, the state, and the regions. Although regional participation was restricted in the initial negotiations between the Commission and the central government, it was more significant than national participation in the operationalization phase and overwhelming in the monitoring phase (Nanetti 1996: 85-6).

Conversely, in the three smaller countries with only regional administrative regional planning districts (Greece and Portugal) or monitoring districts (Ireland), national ministries dominated the CSF process. Importantly, however, 'here too the networks of territorial and institutional relations became more complex and at the same time more articulated and differentiated' (Nanetti 1996: 86). Participation in the implementation of CFS created a 'bottom up demand for more' which conflicted with the centralized management structure, particularly where subnational authorities sought informal but direct contacts with Commission officials. However, some smaller authorities were 'often overwhelmed' by the tasks involved with CSF implementation and drew more readily on support from national ministries. Even here, though, evidence suggested that these authorities were quick to make demands for strengthening their administrative capacity (Nanetti 1996: 86).

Overall, and despite national governments retaining almost exclusive powers of negotiation with the Commission over policy formation, Nanetti (1996: 86-87) concluded that 'the early years of implementation of the first CSFs proved the slow but steady emergence of the regional level as the new institutional partner of the Commission in the operationalization and monitoring of broad-based development policies'.

Partnership in Germany
Anderson (1996) suggested that the German 'spatial-federal' system, which endows its regional governments with considerable autonomy, might lead one to expect a significant reordering of centre–periphery relations from the partnership requirements of the 1988 reform: 'the Länder, in contrast to their counterparts in regionalized and unitary member states, are well positioned to compete for EU funds and to engage the Commission as full-fledged partners in the formulation and implementation of cohesion policy' (Anderson 1996: 163).

However, while aspects of the 1988 reform had a significant impact on Germany prior to unification in 1990, 'neither the federal nor the regional governments sought to reformulate the relationships they cultivated with one another' (Anderson 1996: 163). After 1990, the impact of structural policy became less clear, with the process of unification impacting on domestic regional policy and territorial relations at the same time. Moreover, unification itself 'created a new territorial constituency in Germany, one that has had the opportunity, the desire, and the means to avail itself of Commission resources' (Anderson 1996: 164).

Prior to 1988, EC regional policy had little impact on subnational actors in Germany. Three factors explained this: first, the dominant position of the Council of Ministers at EU level and the resulting national government monopoly relations with the Commission at the implementation stage. Secondly, the sums Germany received prior to unification were relatively modest, generating little attraction for sub-national actors. Thirdly, the funds Germany received were used to refinance projects already approved for domestic regional assistance, thus limiting the EC impact on development. As a result, 'the federal government faced a dearth of EC-inspired challenges from below to its control over the domestic network during the 1970s' (Anderson 1996: 169).

The administrative changes of 1988 reform had little impact on the distribution of influence between the federal government and the regions. For some time, the *Länder* had played a key role in adminis-trating domestic regional policy. While EC structural policy generally had increased the demands of subregional actors for assistance, there was 'little evidence' that the partnership principle specifically had 'contributed to a shift in preferences, objectives or even basic patterns of interaction at the national–regional nexus' (Anderson 1996: 174).

Following unification, the five new *Länder* were given Objective 1 status from 1991. This brought with it the requirements of structural programming, including the negotiation of a CSF and the development of a monitoring committee bringing together EC, federal, regional and local actors to implement the priorities of the CSF. Despite this, the Commission was unable to form the kind of partnerships in the east that had operated relatively smoothly in the west. The explanation was that 'subnational actors in the former GDR simply were not equipped to contribute independently to the partnership requirement, and quite happily relied on Bonn to carry out this onerous, pressurised task' (Anderson 1996: 179).

Partnership in the United Kingdom*

While it was possible to identify general trends in the partnership arrangements set up to administer the funds after 1988, different 'regions' of the UK experienced different levels of success in develop-ing effective partnerships. One common thread in all regions, however, was the dominant role played the central government through its func-

---

* References to local authority and other officials cited in this section taken from Bache 1996.

tional ministries in England and territorial ministries in Scotland and Wales. A survey of local authority experiences of the partnership arrangements reported that relationships in Scotland were generally better than in England and Wales (for details, see Bache 1996: 243-57; for a summary, see Bache, George and Rhodes 1996: 303-308).

Partnership had a longer history in Scotland than elsewhere and there were perceived advantages in dealing with a single territorial ministry, close to the policy community. As one local authority officer (1995) stated: 'Scotland is a long way from London, with a single government department. It makes a difference when the people you are dealing with are across the road.' In addition, Scottish partnerships pioneered the introduction of independent secretariats for servicing the programme monitoring committees, instead of government departments. However, even in Scotland, many partners found the new arrangements far from satisfactory. Brunskill (1992: 15) argued: 'Many partners felt that part-nership was "more apparent than real" and that often discussions took place between the SO [Scottish Office] and the EC with little regard to the other partners.'

In Wales, the advantages that appeared to stem from a territorial ministry in Scotland were less evident. It was not that the Welsh Office had more authority under the regulations than the Scottish Office, but chose to exercise its authority in a more confrontational manner. As one local authority officer (1995) put it: 'the relationship between the Welsh Office and the other partners is like the relationship between a brick wall and anyone who throws their head against it'. Another sug-gested that 'the Welsh Office has been antagonistic towards the idea of partnership. It is a significantly different situation in Scotland' (local authority officer, 1995).

The structures established after the 1988 gave the Welsh Office a pivotal role:

> Not only is the monitoring committee dominated by the Welsh Office, but the Welsh Office also controls the technical groups which feed the information into a secretariat run by the Welsh Office. The whole pro-cess is very much controlled by the Welsh Office (local authority officer, 1995).

Local authorities and other partners argued that programme committees in Wales should follow the example set in Scotland of being admin-istered by an independent secretariat rather than the government office. This change took place, and with other developments, contributed to improved partnership relations in Wales after 1996.

In England, the experience of partnerships differed across regions. Aspects of the partnership arrangements were viewed positively, but few partners doubted that central government controlled key decisions. This included 'ring-fencing' a proportion of the structural funds to finance its own measures. Also controversial was the government's control over committee memberships. In one English region, choice of local authority representation was taken over by government regional office. Those selected were regarded in local government as 'senior generalists rather than structural fund specialists' (Bache, George and Rhodes 1996: 307). This held up the prospect of it being more difficult successfully to challenge government policy within the partnerships.

It was noticeable in comments from English local authority officers that relations with the regional offices of central government were better than with their Whitehall counterparts. As with Scotland, proximity was considered important, leading to 'day-to-day' contact. This relationship was enhanced by an increasing number of secondees from local authorities and other partners working in government regional offices. The secondee system seemed appreciated by all concerned as a good way of increasing understanding of the problems faced by the different partners (Bache 1996: 256).

Finally, in the UK, central government control over the membership of structural fund committees meant the continued exclusion of trade union participation. The exclusion of trade unions undermined the key structural fund objective of greater social and economic cohesion, in particular by preventing employees from highlighting 'the practical experience of large sections of the workforce in industries facing structural change' (Pillinger 1994: 31).

Explaining Variations across Member States

The implementation of the partnership principle varied considerably across Member States. Actors at different levels—national, subnational and supranational—controlled different resources in different Member States, influencing their ability to shape policy implementation within the framework set by EU-level agreements. In short, partnership in principle applied equally to all Member States, whereas partnership in practice was implemented unevenly. Moreover, the UK study in particular showed significant variations in the operation of partnerships within a Member State.

Marks (1996a) argued that variations in the involvement of actors at different levels also varied with the particular stage of the implementation process. Four stages were identified: (1) the formulation of national or, more commonly, regional development plans that become the basis of negotiation with the Commission; (2) the transformation of regional development plans into formal contracts allocating resources (CSFs); (3) the negotiation of CSFs into Operational Programmes which detail the projects to be funded to achieve CSF priorities; and (4) the implementation and monitoring of Operational Programmes (Marks 1996a: 398-406).

In commenting on national variations, Marks (1996a: 406-17) reached four main conclusions in explaining the pattern of political influence over the four stages: first, that the influence of subnational actors in all Member States is characterized by the same ordinal hierarchy, stage 4 → stage 3 → stage 1 → stage 2. In other words, subnational influence in all Member States is greatest in the implementation and monitoring of Operational Programmes, and least in the negotiation of CSFs with the Commission (see Table 5.1).

Secondly, Marks argued that variations in political influence between different actors are greater across countries than within them. Despite this (point three), the role of subnational governments in structural policy is more than a simple reflex of prior domestic arrangements. So, for example, structural programming may have some effect on domestic territorial relations as a whole. Finally, the role of the Commission depends, in the first place, on its relative financial role: the greater the amount the EU provided relative to domestic structural spending, the greater the political influence of the Commission (Marks 1996a: 406-17).

In terms of the consequences of structural programming for territorial relations within Member States, Marks noted that any dramatic changes would not be immediate. However, rising expectations among subnational actors and increased demands for increased political influence resulting from involvement in structural policy might be a good indicator of future impact on territorial relations within Member States. Here, again, the pattern was uneven. For example, in Ireland, the gatekeeper role of central government was undermined, while in Greece there was no substantial impact on territorial relations. In Belgium and Spain, the partnership arrangements contributed to existing pressures for regionalization, while in France, Germany and the UK the arrangements did not

Table 5.1: Political Influence in Structural Programming 1989–93

	Stage	Central Government	Regional Governments	Local Governments	European Commission
BELGIUM	S1	weak	moderate	strong	moderate
	S2	weak	strong	insignificant	moderate
	S3	weak	strong	insignificant	moderate
	S4	weak	moderate to strong	weak to strong	moderate to strong
FRANCE	S1	strong	weak	weak	insignificant
	S2	strong	insignificant	insignificant	weak
	S3	strong	weak	weak	moderate
	S4	strong	weak	weak	weak
GERMANY	S1	moderate	strong	weak	insignificant
	S2	moderate	strong	insignificant	weak
	S3	insignificant	strong	moderate	weak
	S4	insignificant	strong	moderate	moderate
GREECE	S1	strong	weak	insignificant	weak
	S2	strong	insignificant	insignificant	moderate
	S3	strong	weak	insignificant	moderate
	S4	strong	weak	moderate	moderate
IRELAND	S1	strong	insignificant	weak	weak
	S2	strong	insignificant	insignificant	moderate
	S3	strong	insignificant	insignificant	moderate
	S4	strong	weak	moderate	moderate
ITALY	S1	strong	weak to moderate	insignificant	weak
	S2	strong	weak	insignificant	moderate
	S3	moderate	weak to moderate	weak	moderate
	S4	moderate	weak to moderate	weak	moderate
SPAIN	S1	strong	moderate to strong	insignificant	weak
	S2	strong	weak	insignificant	moderate
	S3	strong	strong	insignificant	moderate
	S4	strong	strong	insignificant	moderate
UK	S1	strong	insignificant	insignificant	insignificant
	S2	strong	insignificant	insignificant	weak
	S3	strong	insignificant	weak	weak
	S4	strong	insignificant	weak	moderate

Source: Marks 1996a: 407.

substantially shift the balance of resources between domestic actors (see Marks 1996a: 414-17).

Partnerships in Community Economic Development Programmes
The CED priority in UK structural fund programmes for 1994–96 provided a new experiment in EC regional policy. It had two strands: to concentrate resources on small areas of exceptional deprivation within eligible regions; and to engage the local community—residents and businesses—in the process of regeneration. CED was a direct response to problems of economic and social exclusion from mainstream activities.

The CED priority originated in the UK Unit in Commission DG XVI and the first experiment was in the Merseyside Objective 1 programme for 1994–99. The Merseyside experiment was contained in a measure called 'Pathways to Integration', the success of which was 'crucially dependent on involvement of local residents and businesses. Local residents and firms should be the key players in designing, setting up and monitoring the initiatives, with assistance from local councils and other groups' (Tofarides forthcoming). By placing local communities at the centre of the initiative, the CED priority was a 'bottom-up' attempt at regeneration in contrast with the norm of 'top-down' approaches led by state actors at national, supranational or even subnational level. CED enshrined a new approach to partnership, including for the first time local residents and business representatives as key partners in addition to existing agencies. CED would seek to develop both new institutional capacities and those of individuals previously excluded from decision-making. The positive response to the CED initiative in Merseyside encouraged DG XVI to spread the experiment further in UK programmes for 1994–96 and subsequently to other Member States for the 1997–99 programming period.

Early research findings provided a mixed picture of the success of the CED experiment, with some 'top-down' conditions frustrating 'bottom-up' aspirations. The match-funding requirement in particular provided a major obstacle, making local residents dependent on large organizations for financial support (Bache 1998). Nonetheless, the CED approach was an important experiment in attempting to shift the balance between top-down and bottom-up, which, as the House of Lords (1997a: 24) noted, 'lies too near the "top" with bodies geographically and politically remote from the ground'.

Partnership: Conclusion

The introduction and implementation of the partnership principle was arguably the most significant development in regional policy after its creation in 1975. While predicated on the argument that partnerships improve policy effectiveness, there were obvious political implications from these 'administrative' arrangements. In particular, the partnership principle meant the formal involvement in decision-making of subnational actors in Member States where their role had previously been consultative. The principle has challenged traditional hierarchical relationships between central government and localities.

Regional structural fund partnerships have stimulated the development of policy communities, characterized by 'stability of relationships, continuity of a highly restrictive membership based on shared service delivery responsibilities and insulation from other networks and invariably from the general public' (Rhodes 1992: 78). State and non-state partners meet on a routine basis in the programme monitoring committees and subcommittees and in between are required to maintain regular contact to ensure that partnership decisions are implemented. There is a shared objective among all officials at this level of implementation to 'get the money spent'.

Nonetheless, relations within structural fund partnerships are often asymmetrical. In particular, structural fund regulations gave central governments a high degree of control over the key political and financial resources within regional partnerships. Other actors were able to mobilize political, financial and informational resources to different degrees in different Member States and even within Member States. The outcome was that, while structural fund partnerships challenged existing territorial relations within Member States, this challenge was met with different degrees of resistance and with different outcomes. In centralized Member States where national government actively sought to play a gatekeeper role over the political impact of the new arrangements, such as in the UK, it met with considerable success. There was sufficient scope within the requirements for national governments to dominate partnerships, where it had the will to do so. Here, subnational actors were mobilized, but not necessarily empowered. In more decentralized Member States, subnational authorities—normally regional governments—were better placed to take advantage of the opportunities provided by the partnership requirement. In 1998, the Commission stated that, 'While significant progress has been made in involving regional authorities, in particular where regionalization is least developed, the involvement of local authorities most directly concerned...is still very patchy' (1998b: 11).

CED was a unique experiment within partnerships. For the first time, the Commission sought the direct involvement in policy-making of the local community as residents and as business people, illustrating concern with *political inclusion* in addition to more obvious economic and social objectives. Here, this broadening of partnerships was more a challenge to local rather than central government in the UK. While often an ally of the Commission in challenges to central government power from 'above and below', local government itself faced a similar challenge. Against a context of sustained public disaffection with political institutions and apathy towards local politics illustrated by low turnouts for elections, the model of local governance in the UK was challenged from without to add to existing challenges from within.

In terms of structural fund partnerships generally, and CED in particular, the real measure of their impact cannot be taken so soon into the experiment. Moreover, other policies and processes have encouraged decentralization and devolution of power before and during the structural fund partnership experiments. While this devolution 'cannot be said to be either substantial or irreversible', it has been 'consistent with a wide-spread demand, not confined to the Member States of the EU15, for greater local and regional autonomy' (House of Lords 1997a: 24). At a minimum, therefore, by 1997 the partnership principle for administering the structural funds had at least *contributed to* the debate and process of decentralization of power in EC Member States.

Additionality

The focus of this section is on the implementation of the additionality principle in the UK, although the implementation of additionality in other Member States is also considered briefly. The focus is on the UK for two reasons: first, because, after 1988, the Commission singled out the UK as the only Member State to continue breaching the principle. The former Commissioner for Regional Policy Bruce Millan stated:

> This was a specific British problem. In other member states there were difficulties getting information. In some instances the information was not kept in the right form. But these were not matters of principle. Those easiest to deal with were the poorest member states where the whole country was covered (Millan, quoted in Bache 1996: 274).

Secondly, the additionality problem in the UK culminated in a dispute over the RECHAR programme. The outcome of this dispute was taken as significant for theoretical developments over EU policy-making (Marks 1993; Pollack 1995).

Additionality in the UK: The RECHAR Dispute
RECHAR was the first significant Community Initiative (CI) programme introduced after the 1988 reform of the structural funds. It provided ECU 320 million for economic development projects in the declining coalfield areas of Belgium, France, Germany, Portugal, Spain and the UK. The programme provided the Commission with the opportunity to confront recalcitrant Member States over the principle of additionality, with the UK a particular target. The Commission used its control over CIs to announce the introduction of RECHAR after the UK government had set out its public expenditure plans for the three-year financial period that the new programme would cover. As such, the government would have to make changes to its public expenditure plans to accommodate RECHAR additionally or be exposed to charges of blatant non-compliance with the 1988 structural fund regulations.

Despite the announcement of the RECHAR programme, the government made no changes to its arrangements for implementing additionality. It claimed to have anticipated the announcement of the RECHAR programme and to have already made the necessary adjustments to its public expenditure plans. Commissioner for Regional Policy, Bruce Millan, was not convinced and refused to release the UK share of RECHAR (at over ECU 150 million, almost half the total fund) until the UK government demonstrated that it was providing additionality. Meanwhile, RECHAR funds were released to qualifying regions in other Member States.

Almost a year into the dispute, Michael Heseltine, Secretary of State for the Environment, wrote to the Secretaries of State for Scotland and Wales in December 1991, stating:

> We need to take action to improve the public expenditure treatment of European Regional Development Fund monies coming to UK regions. Our present arrangements fail to ensure that local authorities and other bodies are able to spend the ERDF receipts to which they are entitled (Heseltine 1991: 1).

With Cabinet divisions fuelling increasingly critical media coverage, the government came under pressure from Conservative backbenchers to resolve the dispute. A general election had to be held in 1992 and a number of Conservative MPs held marginal seats in coalfield areas affected. The pressure on the government increased when Commissioner Millan announced that, without a solution, European aid for other parts of the UK might be withheld, potentially affecting more marginal Conservative seats.

After a year-long dispute in which the Commission received full support from the local authorities affected, and with press leaks of a Cabinet split on the issue, the government agreed to meet the Commission's requirements. In February 1992, with the announcement of a general election date imminent, the government set out its position in a letter to Commissioner Millan. This stated:

> In future, published expenditure plans will show forecast ERDF receipts separately for each expenditure programme which receives them. There will be a change also in the public expenditure survey rules, so that public expenditure cover will be made available for those forecast receipts (Kerr 1992: 1).

The Commission immediately announced its intention to release the outstanding RECHAR monies and withdrew its threat to withhold other funds. (For a full account of the RECHAR dispute, see Bache 1996: 151-88.)

Assessing the RECHAR Dispute
The combined efforts of the Commission and UK local authorities provided a unique challenge to central government control over the implementation of the structural funds in the UK. Early accounts of the RECHAR dispute suggested the outcome had significant implications for conceptualizing EU regional policy-making. In particular, Marks (1993: 403) argued:

> Several aspects of the conflict—the way in which local actors were mobilised, their alliance with the Commission, and the effectiveness of their efforts in shifting the government's position—confirm the claim that structural policy has provided subnational governments and the Commission with new political resources and opportunities in an emerging multilevel policy arena.

Yet, while the activity of the unique alliance between the Commission and local authorities illustrated new political resources and opportunities arising from the 1988 reform of the structural funds, their importance could only be fully assessed when the policy changes they had apparently secured had been implemented.

A study of the implementation of the new arrangements for providing 'additionality' (Bache 1996) found that the introduction of 'additional' spending consents (Supplementary Credit Approvals or 'SCAs') to local authorities for European grants after 1992 was compensated for by a reduction in existing spending consents from central government (Basic Credit Approvals or 'BCAs'). In short, genuine additionality had again been denied. Table 5.2 illustrates the situation as it affected English local authorities.

Table 5.2: DoE Credit Approvals to English Local Authorities 1990–95

(£ million)	1990/91	1991/92	1992/93	1993/94	1994/95
BCAs	135.5	169.2	95.4	15.0	zero
SCAs (ERDF)	25.0	45.0	45.0	151.0	170.0

Source: DoE 1991–95.

So, as Marks argued, the RECHAR dispute was indeed characterized by the emergence of a unique alliance between the Commission and subnational actors working to secure a change in the government's policy on additionality. However, the significance of this achievement was revealed to be more apparent than real when the new policy was implemented. The administrative arrangements had changed, but the UK government view of ERDF payments as reimbursement for its contribution to the EU budget had apparently not, and all the evidence suggested that the government had continued its policy of using ERDF payments to displace its own spending in the regions. (For a full discussion, see Bache 1996.)

Additionality in Other Member States

At the beginning of 1992, the Department of the Environment (1992a) produced an internal memo for the Secretary of State on the implementation of additionality in other Member States. The report identified three broad approaches to handling Community receipts, the third of which was closest to the UK situation.

The first approach, which paired together France and Germany, was characterized by the inclusion in the national public expenditure systems of 'direct budgetary lines' for ERDF receipts. This meant that, unlike the case of the UK, anticipated ERDF receipts could not be mixed with other budget lines and thus central government grants were not seen to be reduced by the amount of such receipts as they were in the UK. It was suggested that

> the French further protect themselves from Commission accusations of non-additionality by organising the national resources spent on opera-tional programmes into distinct multi-annual programmes. The size of these commitments of national resources are determined before likely levels of ERDF receipts are known. To this extent ERDF receipts in France are genuinely additional (DoE 1992a: Annexe B).

However, the report noted differences in the French and German sys-tems:

> The German system is closer to our own than the French in that govern-ment spending may be reduced in order to cover increased EC receipts. Such cuts are not necessarily attributed to the budget of the Department benefiting from the receipts (DoE 1992a: Annexe B).

Anderson (1996) argued that, before 1988, EC funds were used 'almost exclusively' for refinancing projects approved for domestic regional funds. The absence of additionality in Germany before 1988 'meant the absence of Commission impact on German regional objec-tives and federal relations' (Anderson 1996: 190). This situation changed 'dramatically' after 1988: 'Via Community Programmes and the like, the Commission now had the capacity to upset the delicate distributional balance among problem regions' and made the Federal Ministry of Economics 'concerned about losing control over develop-ment and expenditure priorities, not to mention the procedures attend-ing development' (Anderson 1996: 190).

Grouped together by the DoE's 'second approach' to additionality were Denmark and Portugal. The report was unequivocal in stating that Denmark operated a system of 'genuine additionality'. There was no mechanism for reducing public expenditure in anticipation of EC contributions, and EC receipts went directly to 'the appropriate recipi-ents'. However, it was noted that Denmark received only a relatively small amount in ERDF grants and, as such, could afford to operate this system without significant impact on public expenditure levels. In Por-tugal also, genuine additionality appeared to be provided, albeit through a different mechanism. Here, structural fund receipts were treated as being outside the state budget and were not regarded as part of public expenditure. The funds were distributed through a separate accounting

procèduie, which meant that 'once the annual national budget is passed
by Parliament it is difficult to re-allocate resources so as to take account
of higher than anticipated EC receipts' (DoE 1992a: Annexe B).

The third approach outlined was the position taken in Spain. This
was identified as being closest to that of the UK government. Here, 'the
amount by which EC receipts are allowed to increase public spending
beyond planned budget limits is strictly controlled…budget calculations are made on the basis of combined totals of estimated EC receipts
and national contributions' (DoE 1992a: Annexe B). The whole tone of
the DoE memo was critical of the Treasury-led government position.
The comparative study, although, by the admission of the authors, a
'limited view', led to the conclusion that 'the UK position, whilst not
dissimilar to that of Spain, remains comparatively isolated within the
Community' (DoE 1992a: Annexe B).

The Politics of Additionality
The intervention of the European Commission over the RECHAR programme was necessary to change UK government policy on additionality. Previously, the resources available to central government allowed
it to determine the domestic arrangements for implementation of the
additionality principle, despite opposition from the most important
other domestic actor: local government. Within the UK system, local
authorities were dependent on central government for their constitu-
tional position, their financial power and, to a considerable degree, for
political legitimacy. While local authority practitioners commanded
informational resources necessary for successful policy implementation, these alone were not decisive in shaping implementation policy.
The decision to withhold structural fund payments brought the Commission firmly into the domestic network, bringing with it substantial
resources to be used in the bargaining process.

Coming out of the 1988 reform negotiations, both the UK government and the Commission had reason to be satisfied with the agreement
on additionality. The UK government had what seemed to be an
exemption clause, as it did not appear likely to benefit from 'increases
in the appropriations' in the forthcoming programme period. Moreover,
negotiations for the 1993 reform would be under way before the 1988
programme period had ended and thus there would be another opportunity to renegotiate any 'difficult' regulations. For its part, the Commission had a new form of words which at the very least, justified

taking a closer look at the implementation of additionality in Member States. Moreover, its control over Community Initiative programmes agreed in the 1988 reform provided it with a surprise weapon. It was not coincidental that the 1993 reform increased Council control over CIs.

If the Commission had brought new financial resources to an existing asymmetrical central–local dispute, the support it received from local authorities throughout the dispute greatly enhanced the unelected Commission's resources of political legitimacy. This mutual support was particularly important because the Commission was to some extent able to appear to the public as a supranational actor with no obvious agenda in UK central–local relations. For those in the media sympathetic to the local authority–Commission arguments, this perception was one worth maintaining and an important one in sustaining political legitimacy. This unique alliance was sustained by the formal linkage of a shared policy objective, but enhanced by good informal relations between key personnel on both sides. Good relations existed between Commission officials in DG XVI and officials and politicians in local government, fostered during a period of frosty relations between centre and locality in the UK. In addition, Commissioner Millan had considerable party political linkages within the local authorities affected: he was a former Labour Secretary of State for Scotland, and the local authorities affected were overwhelmingly Labour-controlled. It may not have been coincidental that, according to one local government secondee to a government regional office in England, the Scottish region of the Coalfield Communities Campaign was regarded in government circles as the most effective arm of the lobbying organization during the RECHAR dispute (Bache 1996). Certainly, these good informal relations provided easier access to the Commissioner for the local authorities involved than they might have expected with a Commissioner from another country or with a former Conservative minister from the UK.

Informal relations were also important in the filtering of information between central government and local authorities during the RECHAR dispute. While officially locked in stalemate, communication between central and local government took place on a regular basis informally. Through these informal channels local authority personnel received information about the government's position on additionality beyond that contained in official statements. Thus, while officially the government promoted an aura of calm concern about the dispute, unofficially senior ministers were furious about the action of local authorities and the Commission and let this be known. By facilitating a fuller understanding of the position of all sides, informal channels were an advantage to all involved and thus were maintained as an unofficial way of striving for progress in the RECHAR dispute when none was being made in official meetings.

The February 1992 agreement between the government and the Commission struck the balance sought by both sides. Immediately, it meant the Commission conceded crucial financial and political resources to the government. The Commission's release of all outstanding funds withdrew the uncertainty of the financial implications of the dispute, while at the same time signalling that the government's political legitimacy over the implementation of additionality was restored. The agreement reached between the government and the Commission neutralized the criticism of Mr Heseltine and others within the Conservative Party and also that from local authorities, thus immediately limiting the potential electoral damage of the dispute.

Both the context and significance of the February 1992 agreement were much clearer with hindsight than they appeared to most observers and many practitioners at the time. Rather than a clear victory for the Commission, the agreement amounted to a short-term public embarrassment for the government and some short-term financial concessions. The government did not interpret the agreement as a binding commitment to provide additionality but as a deal that allowed it and the Commission relief from the pressures the dispute brought.

Thus, while the dispute did illustrate the Commission's ability to galvanize available political and financial resources to some effect, even at the 'high point' of its control of these resources, the policy outcome remained unclear. The Commission hoped that greater transparency would make it very difficult for the UK government to circumvent additionality regulations in the future. The government knew that the impending general election bought it time in which civil servants could devise a means through which transparency could be provided while maintaining a system through which additionality could be interpreted in line with the agreement with the Commission, but with no impact on overall public spending levels. Alternatively, the problem could have been one faced by a new governing party.

The information forwarded to the Commission by local authorities after the RECHAR dispute provided convincing evidence that the UK government simply substituted expenditure on ERDF projects for domestic expenditure on projects of a similar nature. The Commission believed the UK government breached the additionality principle before 1992 and understood that the spirit of the principle, if not the letter, continued to be ignored afterwards. Despite its efforts, the Commission was ultimately dependent on UK central government for the successful implementation of additionality. After the RECHAR dispute, the issue of additionality fell in the order of Commission priorities and consequently fell from public prominence. The state of the Union meant that other matters were more pressing and the Commission had fewer resources with which to try to force the issue.

The changes introduced by the re-elected Conservative government in June 1992 did not significantly change the UK position on additionality. However, by reducing central government allocations to local authorities to compensate for 'additional' EU grants, the government made it difficult for the Commission to take further action. Cuts to domestic allocations, it argued, were a matter for national government and not for the Commission. Despite subsequent complaints from local authorities to the Commission about the lack of effective additionality, the Commission made noises about further action in 1993, but there were no significant developments. The Commission's focus had moved on in the context of the post-Maastricht ratification crisis, and so did the British Commissioner for Regional Policy, Bruce Millan, who had been particularly keen to tackle the additionality problem.

Implementing Environmental Provisions

Despite provisions in the 1988 reform attempting to deal with the environmental threat posed by structural fund operations, environmental concerns in practice took a low priority. The rhetoric of the reform was not matched by effective operational structures for assessing the environmental impact of operations. The Commission was inadequately resourced to perform the task, with only six Commission officials dedicated to monitoring this aspect of operations across all Member States. Moreover, Member States were reluctant to supply full information on environmental implications and the Commission had no clear powers under the regulations to insist that governments comply with the request in the regulations (Scott 1995: 82).

Non-governmental environmental organizations, which had mobilized around a 'European Campaign for the Reform of the Structural Funds', were equally powerless to ensure adequate implementation of environmental requirements. Scott (1995: 83) noted that these groups were 'entirely excluded from national or regional monitoring committees in theory as well as practice—committees which at any rate do not have an explicit environmental remit'. The various stages of the planning process for structural fund operations took place without public consultation, allowing no additional input to that provided by partners selected by national governments.

Through the Environmental Impact Assessment Directive of 1985, Member States held the primary responsibility for ensuring sustainable development through structural fund operations. However, the effectiveness of this directive in relation to structural fund operations was constrained by its limited coverage of projects and by the limited effect of assessment results. Coverage was restricted to a narrow range of projects that the directive required for assessment and also restricted by a focus on the impact of individual projects rather than on the cumulative impact of a series of related measures (see Scott 1995: 84-88). In terms of the effect of assessment results, the directive contained 'no more than a vague and hopeful exhortation that the environmental insights revealed as a result of assessment be reflected in the decisions of the competent authorities' (Scott 1995: 8).

The 1993 structural fund regulations sought to strengthen the Commission's powers for regulating the behaviour of Member States in ensuring respect for the environment. However, the provisions were criticized. Scott (1995: 94-96) made a number of important criticisms: first, that the nature and scope of the obligations provided in the 1993 reform were so vague that they left 'substantial discretion' in the hands of member states. Secondly, there was still a need for environmental assessment to be strategic, rather than project-based. Thirdly, the amendments failed to take account of the limited effectiveness of the Environmental Impact Assessment Directive and provided no concrete power to national designated environmental authorities. Finally, the new regulations failed to open up the structural fund planning process to non-governmental organizations. In short, the regulations 'failed to respond adequately to the environmental challenge inherent in the implementation of the structural funds' (Scott 1995: 97).

Implementation: Conclusion

The 1988 reform of the structural funds provided a classic illustration of how EU-level agreements could be frustrated at the policy implementation stage. The principles of partnership and additionality were implemented very differently by Member States in practice. Yet the partnership principle remained key to the Commission's pursuit of an effective regional policy. In its proposals for the 1998 reform, the Commission argued for a *deepening* of partnerships so that partners would be more involved throughout the process of financing from the structural funds. Perhaps more significantly, the Commission noted the 'very patchy' involvement of local authorities, environmental authorities and other bodies (the social partners, local voluntary organizations, non-governmental bodies, etc.) who were 'dealing with matters of major concern to the Community, such as employment, sustainable development and equal opportunities for men and women' (Commission 1998b: 11). The next chapter considers the Commission's proposals for the 1999 reform.

In terms of theoretical developments, perhaps the main lesson from the implementation of the 1988 reform was that

> Analysts who want to predict developments in EU cohesion policy from the great bargains risk overlooking the ambivalence in the regulations; the active role of the European Commission, national administrations, and subnational actors in exploiting these ambiguities; and the effects of policy learning (Hooghe 1996b: 119).

In particular, where national governments are determined to resist unwanted outcomes from developments at EU level, they will carry their 'gatekeeper' role over into the policy implementation stage.

In a study of the implementation of the principles of the 1988 reform in the UK, it has been argued that existing explanations of the EU policy process would be strengthened by analysing the impact of implementation on policy outcomes (Bache 1996). For those in the pluralist tradition, there was much evidence of multi-level involvement in the implementation of EC regional policy in the UK, but the extent to which it constituted multi-level governance was unclear. Certainly, in relation to the principles of additionality and partnership, analysis of policy outcomes suggested that the gatekeeper role of UK national government was played with some success at the implementation stage. For intergovernmentalists, this research suggested that, where the gatekeeper notion was useful in describing the behaviour of national governments in EU policy-making, it makes sense to refer to an *extended gatekeeper* that can operate at all stages of the policy process, including implementation.

6 |

Recent Developments and Future Prospects

Introduction

This chapter considers some recent developments in EC regional policy and considers its future prospects. It begins by outlining some of the achievements of the structural funds and the Cohesion Fund as detailed in the Commission's First Cohesion Report of 1996. The focus here is largely on the economic impact of EC cohesion policies, with the political impact dealt with more fully in the final chapter. The second section of this chapter deals with the Commission's recent proposals for the 1999 reform of the structural funds. The chapter concludes with a brief consideration of the future of EC regional policy, a subject also returned to in the final chapter.

The structural funds and the Cohesion Fund are the main EC policy instruments for achieving economic and social cohesion, an objective made explicit by the SEA. However, Member States and the Commission agree that 'Member State policies are the Union's primary instruments for achieving cohesion' (Commission 1996a: 7). The question is, then, not whether Community policies by themselves are achieving economic and social cohesion but whether they achieve results that would not be achieved by Member State policies alone.

The First Cohesion Report

Article 130b of the Treaty on European Union called for the Commission to

> submit a report to the European Parliament, the Council, the Economic and Social Committee and the Committee of the Regions every three years on the progress made to achieving economic and social cohesion and the manner in which the various means provided for in this Article have contributed to it.

Subsequently, in 1996, the European Commission published its *First*

Report on Economic and Social Cohesion. The report aimed to address four main questions:

- Have economic and social disparities between Member States, regions and social groups narrowed over time, leading to an improvement in 'the overall harmonious development' of the Union?

- What have been the role and the achievements of Member States' policies in this respect?

- How have the Union's non-structural policies responded to the Treaty obligation to take account of cohesion objectives?

- What has been the effect of the Union's structural policies? (Commission 1996a: 5).

The main concern here is with the last of these questions; however, the other questions will be dealt with briefly.

Social and Economic Fortunes

The Cohesion Report stated that, in the period 1983–95, disparities in income per head between Member States 'narrowed significantly', primarily due to the progress made by the 'Cohesion Four' countries—Spain, Portugal, Greece and Ireland. These countries saw their average incomes per head rise from 66 per cent to 74 per cent of the Community average over the period. Of these, Ireland performed best with an annual average growth rate of 4.5 per cent between 1983 and 1995. However, while income disparities between Member States narrowed, disparities between EU *regions* remained largely unchanged. For the 25 best-off regions, income per head rose from 140 per cent to 142 per cent of the EU average; while for the 25 poorest regions it rose from 53 per cent to 55 per cent. Figures provided after the Cohesion Report revealed that the EC's richest region, Hamburg (Germany), was more than four times wealthier in terms of GDP per capita than the poorest region Ipeiros (Greece). Almost one in four EU regions was below three-quarters of the EU average in terms of GDP per capita and two regions were under half the EU average (Ipeiros and the French overseas departments, taken as a whole) (Eurostat 1998). Moreover, in the decade to 1995, regional income disparities widened *within* all Member States in which they were measured, with the exception of the Netherlands.

The experience across Member States with regard to unemployment was mixed, but generally poor. For example, despite Ireland's remarkable growth rate, employment grew by only 0.2 per cent in the period 1983–93 (Commission 1996a: 5). The incidence of unemployment across EU regions became more uneven. In the period 1983–93, unemployment in the 25 regions with the lowest rates fell from 4.8 per cent to 4.6 per cent, while there was a dramatic increase in the 25 regions with the highest rates from 17.2 per cent to 22.4 per cent. The problem of unemployment affected weaker social groups disproportionately. Young people, women and people without qualifications were particularly affected by unemployment and almost half (49 per cent) of those unemployed had been out of work for over a year. Finally, regional differences in unemployment rates *within* many Member States increased over the decade to 1995, the notable exception being the UK (Commission 1996a: 5-6).

The Role and Achievements of Member State Policies
As noted above, Member States and the Commission agree that domestic policies are the main instruments for achieving cohesion in the EU. While the Community budget accounts for approximately 1.2 per cent of EU GDP, domestic public spending accounts for between 40 per cent and 60 per cent of national GDP. Inter-regional transfers within Member States take place through public expenditure and taxation. A study of seven countries found that net transfers amount to 4 per cent of the GDP of donor regions and 8 per cent of recipient regions, reducing regional income disparities by 20–40 per cent (Commission 1996a: 6).

The Contribution of Community Policies
There are 'wide differences' in the contribution of different Community policies to the objective of cohesion. Social policies have enhanced the process of integration and cohesion, particularly in relation to labour law, health and security at work, free movement of people and equal opportunities for men and women. In contrast, while the single market programme was claimed to make a positive contribution to employment cohesion, it was noted that 'the reduction of external protection needs to be accompanied by internal economic adjustment'. High tariff industries accounted for almost half of employment in Portugal and Greece, and the four cohesion countries were generally vulnerable to negative impacts from trade liberalization (Commission 1996a: 7-8).

The Effects of EU Structural Policies

The Commission (1996a: 9-10) claimed that, through the creation of Objective 1 regions, the 1988 reform of the structural funds 'significantly increased their redistributive effect in favour of the less prosperous Member States and regions'. In the programming period 1989–93, the structural funds achieved an overall income equalization (in terms of GDP per head) of 3 per cent, with transfers of 0.3 per cent of EU GDP. It was anticipated that for the programming period 1994– 99, transfers of 0.45 per cent of EU GDP would produce an equaliza- tion effect of 5 per cent. The benefits of financial transfers through the structural funds were not only experienced by the poorer Member States. It was estimated that 30–40 per cent of funding received by poorer Member States returned to the richer ones through purchases of 'know-how' or capital equipment (Commission 1996a: 8-10).

Conclusion

The success, or otherwise, of the structural funds in achieving social and economic cohesion within the EU is difficult to measure. First, the picture presented by regional statistics is confusing: the degree of cohesion achieved depends in part on the indicators used. Secondly, it is difficult to disentangle the effect of the structural funds from other effects, particularly national policies. This is best illustrated in the case of Ireland, which by most indicators has been a success story. In addi- tion to the structural funds, contributory factors to this success include 'the national government's sound macro-economic policies; its empha- sis on human resource development and improved labour relations policies involving the social partners; its inward investment policies; and, importantly, the high quality of the public administration of the country' (House of Lords 1997a: 22). Finally, the extent to which the structural funds have led to a reduction in national regional measures— the additionality issue—casts a further doubt over their net contribution to cohesion. Overall, the economic effects of EU structural and cohe- sion policies have been most visible in the poorer Member States, although the accepted view is that regional disparities within and between member states remain 'unacceptably large' (House of Lords 1997a: 23).

There is a more fundamental critique of EU cohesion policies that argues for a broader conception of development than that measured by the per capita GDP of regions. First, measurements of regional GDP say nothing about the distribution of income *within* regions. Secondly, the focus on GDP as a measure of economic growth assumes 'more equals better' and has little concern with measuring the impact of growth on the quality of life in the regions covered. Alternative development methodologies have shown there is no necessary correlation between quantity and quality in development (Scott 1999: 28-30).

Perhaps of more lasting significance than the uncertain contribution of the structural funds to social and economic cohesion might be the political changes instigated. As noted in the previous chapter, structural policies required the development of subnational structures that have contributed to the devolution of decision-making in Member States and to the involvement of new actors in the political process. The significance of this contribution to political inclusion was summed up well by the House of Lords Select Committee on the European Communities:

> cohesion, we believe, is promoted not only by hard measurable outcomes but also by local participation and the sense of ownership. The value of 'bottom-up' contributions to programmes was brought home to us very forcefully in our visits. The degree of local enthusiasm, the sense of hope for a better quality of life and the conviction that, with local effort and national and EU support, it could be achieved, were palpable (House of Lords 1997a: 24).

The 1999 Reform of the Structural Funds

1999 was set to be a critical year for the development of European regional policy. As well as concluding the current programme period and current EU budgetary period, 1999 would see the probable entrance of a majority of Member States into EMU and would be a critical time for the negotiations to enlarge the EU. Other factors affecting the Community's disadvantaged regions beyond 1999 included the ongoing impact of both the completion of the internal market and of the fourth enlargement to include Austria, Finland and Sweden. Finally, the Treaty of Amsterdam of 1997 included a title on employment indicating a desire by Member States to prioritize the problems of unemployment. As one commentator put it:

> The political climate in which the latest round of regional policy reforms is being negotiated is very different from that surrounding previous exercises over the past decade. After the successive expansion of regional and social funding in 1988 and 1993, the emphasis now is very much on budgetary consolidation (Watson 1998: 16).

Enlargement

When enlargement occurs, it will bring into the EU countries from Central and Eastern Europe with an average GDP per capita typically at around one-third of the existing EU15 average. The impact of enlargement on the future of structural and cohesion policy would depend on a number of factors. Of obvious importance was *when* the first wave of enlargement would take place and *which* countries would be involved. Only when these questions were answered would it be possible to calculate with some accuracy the probable EC contribution to new Member States and the consequent impact on funds available to existing members. The calculation would also have to account for the ability of new entrant countries to absorb EC structural aid without distorting their economies:

> Observation of the operation of the structural funds within the EU15 and the operation of the Phare programme within the CEECs convinces us that recipient countries do not have unlimited capacity either to handle and absorb net inflows of investment funds without damaging economic distortions or to produce the co-financing required (House of Lords 1997a: 28).

It was clear to all concerned that simply to apply the existing structural fund criteria to the new Member States would not be financially practicable for the EU. Under the structural fund regulations for 1994–99, the entire territories of the countries of Central and Eastern Europe would qualify for Objective 1 and Cohesion Fund assistance. Extending the current funds to Poland, Hungary, the Czech Republic and Slovakia would increase the total costs of the funds to approximately ECU 48 billion, and would double the funds if all ten countries of Central and Eastern Europe, Cyprus and Malta became members after 2001 (CURDS 1997: 55).

Thus, to fund the new 'winners' under structural policy, there would inevitably be 'losers'. This had to be accepted by those Member States likely to suffer a reduction in aid. Enlargement had consequences far beyond structural policy, as Commissioner for Regional Policy Monika Wulf-Mathies explained in a speech on the implications of enlargement for the UK:

> The arrangements of the Union are designed to secure peace and democracy. Poverty and political instability in those countries would not only have a negative impact on their direct neighbours its consequences on

internal and external security would be no less felt in the UK (Wulf-
Mathies 1997).

EMU

The probable impact of EMU on the Community's poorer regions is
unclear. The Commission's official position is the impact would be
neutral. Emerson *et al.* (1992: 27) put this argument:

> Neither economic theory nor the current experiences of the least
> favoured and geographically peripheral regions of the Community point
> to a bias in the sense that these regions might systematically profit either
> more or less than from EMU than average. While the economic centre of
> the Community benefits from economies of scale advantages, it is not
> evident that these relative advantages are destined to grow. The least
> favoured regions still have other advantages...

   While accepting that the least favoured regions would have advantages in a monetary union, Armstrong (1997: 7) argued that 'these
benefits will only be enjoyed in the long term. On the other hand, the
burdens monetary union places on the disadvantaged regions will be
felt much more quickly. The costs come first; the benefits come later.'
The burdens on weaker regions were likely to be threefold, resulting
from the loss of exchange rate powers; the effects of the attempts to
meet the Maastricht convergence criteria; and the effect of monetary
union on attainment of the single market (Armstrong 1997: 7).

Other Factors

In addition to the impact of enlargement and EMU, Armstrong (1997)
suggested that a further two factors had implications beyond 1999 for
the economies of existing disadvantaged regions: the single European
market and the fourth enlargement to include Austria, Sweden and
Finland. While the single market legislation had been put in place by
the end of 1992 and the fourth enlargement completed by 1995, the
future impact of these developments could not be ignored because
economies required a significant period of time to adjust. In relation to
the single market, for example, the legislation had been put in place,
but the objective of securing an area 'without internal frontiers in which
the free movement of goods, persons, services and capital is ensured'
had not been completed:

> Removing the internal frontier formalities was the easy bit. Getting rid
> of all the other barriers to trade and the free movement of labour will

take a lot longer, and the corporate restructuring which is also occurring will take longer still (Armstrong 1997: 5-6).

The same comments applied to the effects of the fourth enlargement on disadvantaged regions. In short, future enlargement and EMU would add to the challenges already facing disadvantaged regions from the single market and the 1995 accessions.

Agenda 2000 and the Structural Funds

In July 1997, the European Commission presented a strategy document entitled *Agenda 2000: For a Stronger and Wider Union*. This document described the outlook for the European Union for the early years of the next century. It proposed that social and economic cohesion should remain a 'high priority'. In terms of the structural funds and the Cohesion Fund, the Commission proposed a budget of ECU 275 billion (at 1997 prices) for the period 2000–2006, as compared with ECU 200 billion (at 1997 prices) for 1993–99. ECU 45 billion of this amount would be earmarked for the new Member States (Commission DG XVI 1997: 1).

Simplification and Concentration
The Commission proposed that the current seven priority objectives be reduced to three: two regional objectives, and a horizontal objective for human resources. The coverage of the new Objectives 1 and 2 would be reduced from 51 per cent to between 35 and 40 per cent by 2006. Approximately two-thirds of total funding would continue to be allocated to Objective 1 regions. For the structural funds, the Commission proposed co-financing a single multi-annual programme for each region. The number of Community Initiatives would be limited to three (cross-border, transnational and inter-regional cooperation; rural development; and human resources) and their share of structural fund resources would be reduced to 5 per cent (Commission DG XVI 1997: 1).

Under the new *Objective 1*, the Commission proposed that eligibility be strictly limited to those regions whose per capita GDP was less than 75 per cent of the Community average. The amount of funding to each of these regions would be determined by the size of population, the gap between regional wealth and the EU average and national wealth. Additional support would be provided for those regions with very high unemployment. The new *Objective 2* would assist regions confronted with major economic and social restructuring needs. This would include areas affected by change in the industrial, services or fisheries sectors; rural areas in serious decline; and disadvantaged urban districts. The new *Objective 3* would cover those regions not covered by Objectives 1 and 2. This would be aimed at helping those regions adapt and modernize their systems of education, training and employment. Four types of activity would be promoted: accompanying economic and social change; lifelong education and training systems; active labour market policies to fight unemployment; combating social exclusion (Commission DG XVI 1997: 1-2).

The Cohesion Fund
Agenda 2000 proposed that the Cohesion Fund be kept in its present form after 1999. It would therefore continue to co-finance trans-European transport networks and projects in the environmental field in Member States with a per capita GDP of less than 90 per cent of the EU average. The conditionality principle would be maintained, requiring the countries concerned to maintain their convergence efforts. The financial endowment of the Cohesion Fund for the current Member States would be approximately ECU 3 billion per year at the beginning of the 2000–2006 period (Commission DG XVI 1997: 2).

Providing Structural Support for Enlargement
Agenda 2000 proposed that the structural funds and the Cohesion Fund should support development in potential Member States, 'especially in infrastructure, the environment, the productive sector and human resources'. To facilitate the adaptation of potential Member States to the workings of the structural funds, the Commission proposed the introduction of pre-accession aid of ECU 7 billion from 2000. From accession onwards, structural fund and Cohesion Fund allocations totalling ECU 38 billion would be available to new Member States for the period 2000–2006. By 2006, structural aid for enlargement would represent almost 30 per cent of total EU structural funding (Commission DG XVI 1997: 2-3).

Conclusion
While *Agenda 2000* proposed an absolute increase allocations to structural and cohesion funding for the post-2000 programme period, the

proportion of Community GNP devoted to these would remain constant at 0.46 per cent. Economic growth and more efficient use of resources available would generate the extra resources. The commitment of the bulk of these additional resources to new Member States meant a fall in real terms of funding for the existing EU15 after 2000.

Reform of the Structural Funds for 2000–2006: Proposed Regulations

On 18 March 1998, the Commission presented its proposed regulations for governing the structural funds for the period 2000–2006. These proposals put flesh on the bones of *Agenda 2000*. The proposed reform of the structural funds was centred on three priorities: greater concentration, decentralized and simplified implementation and a strengthening of efficiency and control set against a background of budgetary discipline (Commission 1998a: 2).

The Commission proposed to maintain the four governing principles of the structural funds—partnership, concentration, additionality and programming. However, the partnership principle should be reformed so that the responsibilities of each of the partners would be defined 'so as to implement better the principle of subsidiarity and permit improved application of Article 205, under which the Commission is responsible for implementation of the Community budget' (Commission 1998b: 10). The Commission proposed introducing a fifth principle—efficiency—to reassure people that public money allocated to the structural funds was well used.

Partnership
The Commission argued that 'in practice, there still remains much to be done, both to deepen partnership and to widen it' (1998b: 11). *Deepening* the partnership meant that partners would be involved throughout the process of financing from the structural funds: from the design of strategies to the *ex post* evaluation of assistance. To this end, the Commission proposed that development plans submitted by Member States be accompanied by the opinion of all partners and that the monitoring committees would be more closely involved in programming decisions and in evaluation work. In terms of *broadening* partnerships, the Commission noted the 'very patchy' involvement of some partners (see Chapter 5) and proposed explicit provisions requiring

Member States to guarantee that these partners 'be involved in concertation on the implementation of the Structural Funds at national, regional and local level' (Commission 1998b: 11).

Concentration
The 1998 proposals sought concentration of the structural funds in four ways:

- concentration on three priority objectives and three Community Initiatives;

- concentration on areas of priority assistance that encourage an integrated approach to development rather than a fragmentation of operations, aimed at both regional and national needs and the Community priorities;

- geographical concentration to reduce the proportion of the Community population covered;

- financial concentration to give priority to regions whose development is lacking behind (Commission 1998b: 13).

These proposals largely confirmed the provisions of *Agenda 2000* in terms of how concentration would be achieved (see above). Regions eligible for Objective 1 would account for no more than 20 per cent of the EU population, with the same applying to regions eligible for Objective 2. The Commission confirmed that 'extended transitional support'—six years for Objective 1 and four years for Objective 2—would be available for those regions no longer eligible after the reform, to 'prevent any adverse effects' of the withdrawal of funding.

Programming
The Commission confirmed its commitment to 'integrated strategic programming' for the period after 1999. It proposed that all actions funded under the new objectives and Community Initiatives should be integrated into a single programme at regional level. This would ensure that 'the integrated approach gradually introduced by the 1998 reform would be applied in a much broader and more systematic way' (Commission 1998b: 14).

Additionality
The Commission's 1998 proposals acknowledged that 'verifying addi-

tionality is a complex business, principally because it is carried out for each Objective and because it is difficult to identify eligible expenditure, especially for small geographical areas'. Consequently, the Commission proposed simplifying the procedure for verifying additionality. Here, the principle of 'negotiated additionality' was introduced. The Commission would negotiate with each Member State an agreed level of structural expenditure over the programme period. This would have to be 'at least the same as that achieved during the previous programming period so as to maintain that Member State's effort in those regions' (Commission 1998b: 31). In Objective 1 regions, eligible expenditure would be public structural expenditure and in Objectives 2 and 3 it would be expenditure on active labour market policies. Additionality would henceforth be subject to verification at these geographical levels at the beginning, mid-term and towards the end of the programme period.

Assessing the Commission's Proposals
As with previous EU-level decisions on structural policy, the broad context for reform in 1999 was set largely by the imperatives of economic and monetary union and enlargement. While the four principles of 1988 remained intact, and a fifth principle of 'efficiency' would be added, the Commission's proposals were relatively modest and in some areas hinted at a further renationalization of the funds. 'Simplification', for example, was a clear response to Member State demands. As one former Commission official (1998) put it, 'the member states always want simplification. For member states, this means "we don't want you [the Commission] telling us what to do. We don't want you and your heavy structures about decisions and everything else influencing us.".'

In addition to simplifying procedures, the Commission also intended to take a lesser role in the day-to-day management of the funds. This meant withdrawing officials from involvement in partnership activities below programme monitoring committees, where this had been the practice. In short, the context was not favourable towards major Commission advances on regional policy. EMU was crucial in framing a mood of uncertainty. This was acknowledged in interviews with Commission officials: regional policy was defended as a 'success story', but EMU was seen to have crystallized the issue of sovereignty within Member States, creating a political atmosphere against further integration.

The proposed enlargement of the EU focused the Commission's efforts on concentrating the funds on a smaller proportion of the existing EU15 population. While existing Member States accepted the need for concentration in principle, agreeing which areas would be affected by greater concentration in 1999 would be fiercely contested. Moreover, the proposed regulations suggested that, in addition to determining Objective 1 areas, the Council would also have more control over the designation of Objective 2 areas. While these always had an element of national influence, 'it is clear that Objective 2 is going to be 50 per cent determined by national administrations, according to their own basket of indicators' (ex-Commission official, 1998).

The convergence criteria for monetary union established at Maastricht had provided a loose interpretation of the *additionality* requirement after the 1993 reform. While the principle of *negotiated additionality*, if accepted, appeared to be an improvement on this, its success would depend in large part on what the Commission would be able to negotiate with Member States, most of whom were about to experience the first challenges of monetary union. The Commission proposed taking a specific indicator of additionality for each objective to facilitate more effective monitoring. In short, the Commission believed it had 'found a way of measuring it which will facilitate better contacts between the member states and the Commission...that will improve substantially the implementation of additionality' (Commission official, 1998).

However, by 1998, the Commission's focus on additionality was more with *project additionality* than with the extremely difficult task of securing net additional spending in Member States in the context of pressures from EMU. Project additionality referred to the question of whether the money was spent better through the structural funds than it would have been otherwise: the notion of 'value added'. For now, the more global principle of additionality had fallen from the agenda.

Programming remained a relatively uncontroversial principle of structural funding in 1998. As one Commission official (1998) put it,

> Programming has proven its value. It took quite a long learning process, but I think everyone agrees that programming is the best way to implement the structural funds. The current programmes are much better than the ones at the beginning, but there is still scope for improvement.

One proposal for improvement was to reduce the three-stage programming process to two stages, except for very large allocations. This proposal was likely to be welcomed by Member States.

Partnership remained at the core of Commission thinking and the principle would be strengthened if the proposals for 1999 were accepted. The Commission sought to build on the existing provisions by increasing the emphasis placed on involving the social partners, environmental agencies and other non-governmental organizations involved in social and economic development. In short, the Commission proposal 'makes more clear what the partnership should consist of, without giving an actual list' (Commission official, 1998). The proposals would require Member States to submit the development plans, as before, but each would have the opinion of the wider partnership attached.

The Commission's proposed withdrawal from lower levels of partnership was interpreted in some quarters as a clear sign of Commission retreat and national government advance. To an extent, this was necessary on a practical level with the Commission's human resources already stretched and additional responsibilities coming on board from the potential new members of Central and Eastern Europe. In defence of this withdrawal, Commission officials emphasized that they would still be involved in programme monitoring committees and these would take on a more strategic role than previously. This shift, and more effective monitoring and programme evaluations, would allow the Commission to continue playing an important role in programme outcomes:

> The region will have to produce better information on what has been done, so the annual progress report will have to contain more detailed information. So we will stay away from the lower decision-making level, but the regions will have to justify more what they have done (Commission official, 1998).

In addition, the Commission proposed retaining 10 per cent of the structural funds as a *performance reserve* for it to allocate during the programme period to those regions performing well.

Criticism of this new approach focused in part on the efficacy of programme evaluations:

> It's a nice clean rational exercise and the member states are forced to do things that provide better value for money because the evaluation tells them to. But the evaluations for this round will be out in 2002. It's too late—they are always too late (ex-Commission official, 1998).

This criticism may have been harsh, given the Commission's complementary use of interim evaluations to feed into programme operations
mid-term. However, there were domestic concerns about the new proposals, particularly within the German *Länder*. While the proposals
meant greater subsidiarity, they also implied more work for domestic
authorities.

Despite concerns about a greater domestic workload, the Commission's proposed withdrawal from lower-level decision-making was
likely to be welcomed by national governments. However, the proposed
tightening of partnership requirements was more controversial. On this,
the Commission would face challenges at EU level and beyond. Gatekeepers at national and, in some cases, regional level had resisted the
creation of vertical partnerships between national, subnational and
supranational actors in 1988. The broadening of partnerships horizon-
tally to increase the involvement of various non-governmental actors
would surely again meet a similar response. The first indications from
the CED experiments in the UK suggested the empowerment of new
actors was largely at the behest of existing institutional actors.

The need to reduce the number of *Community Initiatives* to simplify
procedures and reduce duplicative structures was accepted by the
Commission. And, while reduced to three in number, this meant more
resources for each remaining CI. The Commission was confident that
CIs would continue to provide scope for Commission discretion and
innovation. One Commission official (1998) suggested that

> the Commission will be very strong position over the future of Commu-
> nity Initiatives. It will have a more independent role in that you won't
> need member states to recommend CIs as much as you do now. It will be
> able to set up different structures by stepping back from the mainstream
> and stepping into other types of activities.

Negotiating the 1999 Reform

The early exchanges over the Commission's proposed regulations for
the 1999 reform followed the typical pattern of Commission–Council
tussle of previous reform negotiations. In March 1998, the UK President of the Board of Trade suggested that Commissioner Wulf-Mathies
seemed to be 'taking some reassurance in the fact that pretty well every
member state is deeply dissatisfied with her proposals. If I were her I
wouldn't find that reassuring' (Beckett 1998). Germany and the Nether-

lands objected that proposed allocations to the funds were too high. Spain felt it would not receive enough under the proposals, and the UK was concerned about its potential losses from reductions in Objective 2 funding. And, while there was a general consensus among governments that Objective 1 regions should be defined strictly according to the 75 per cent GDP criteria proposed by the Commission, the French and UK governments had concerns about this.

There was again a different view over allocations taken by the likely net payers and net beneficiaries under the proposals. For example, the proposals suggested that the reform would reduce eligible regions in the Netherlands, so the Dutch would receive less while the overall budget increased. The Dutch government hoped to obtain sufficient support from other governments to reduce the proposed budget, which would have a proportionally high impact on their contribution. However, it did not receive the support it wanted—particularly from the German and Austrian governments—so it changed its strategy to one of seeking ways to maximize its allocations.

During the negotiations, a 'safety net' mechanism was agreed for existing Objective 2 regions. This meant that population coverage for the post-1999 programming period could only be reduced in those areas by a maximum of one-third. Certain countries, including the UK, would have lost much more without this mechanism. The UK government also had concerns about the cut-off point of 75 per cent of GDP for Objective 1 areas. Under this, it would probably secure eligibility for two areas—Merseyside and South Yorkshire. However, 'if you had, as we have now, 75 meaning in fact 80, that would mean an enormous increase in the UK population. There are potentially four UK regions in the bracket 75–80' (Commission official, 1998).

The Commission's proposed 'performance reserve' or 'efficiency fund' was controversial within the Council, and disliked in particular by the German government. Other governments were more amenable should the fund be redistributed within areas in all countries so as not to affect the overall distribution between Member States. No Member State disagreed with the principle of 'efficiency'; however, what that would mean in practice was contentious. In addition to opposition over the efficiency fund, there were difficulties in agreeing efficiency criteria. For example, if job creation was accepted as a criterion of efficiency, there was the question of how it would be measured: gross, net, displacement or multiplier. There would also be questions of the trade-off between direct employment measures and indirect, short term and long term measures. As one Commission official (1998) argued, 'You cannot just put it on one measure…you have to find a combination between different measures. It is quite complex. It means more work has to be done on the whole quantification exercise.'

By mid-1998, a number of key issues remained outstanding. With elections in both Germany and the Netherlands later in the year, some of these issues— financial in particular—would not be decided until the outcome of those elections was known. Working groups continued to look at the regulations, trying to make progress, but no one expected any major decisions before the German elections in September 1998.

Conclusion

Assessing the economic impact of the structural funds and the Cohesion Fund is difficult. The indicators reveal a mixed picture and, even where there has been clear economic success, it is unclear to what extent this is the result of EC or national interventions. The issue is further clouded by the uncertainty over what provision Member States would have made for advancing social and economic cohesion in the absence of Community action, particularly as EC assistance has been a reality for a substantial period of time in all but the newest Member States.

Yet, while funding to national structural policies may have reduced over the period of EC assistance, there is no certainty that these reductions would be reinstated should EC funding be withdrawn. National governments under pressure to limit public spending to meet the convergence criteria for monetary union have not been well placed to increase spending on regional development, and there was no immediate prospect of this pressure being lifted following the completion of monetary union in 1999. The reality was that, within each Member State, a substantial number of jobs depended on the structural funds by 1998 and would continue to do so for some time. As such, future allocations and the distribution of funding would continue to be fiercely contested by Member States.

One important criticism of the Commission's initial proposals (*Agenda 2000*) as a response to the economic aspects of cohesion came in two parts. First was the argument that the proposals addressed only one of the 'looming challenges' to disadvantaged regions, that of Eastern enlargement, when 'there are actually four simultaneous effects likely to be at work (the delayed Single Market effects; the delayed Fourth Enlargement effects; and monetary union effects too) (Armstrong 1997: 11). Secondly, and most seriously, the Commission's proposals did not address the existing failures of the structural funds. These criticisms were at least in part applicable to the detailed proposals set out by the Commission in 1998. For example, it was argued that concentrating assistance on only 35 per cent of the population would not solve the problem of geographical concentration 'since this will inevitably deny assistance to those localities within the disadvantaged regions which have the best growth prospects' (Armstrong 1997: 12).

If it was unclear what the economic impact of the 1998 proposals would be, it was equally uncertain what political significance they would have, although early signs indicated at least a partial renationalization of EC regional policy. The proposals on simplification and concentration were part renationalization and partly a redefinition of roles to improve accountability, particularly financial. Concessions, such as the transitional arrangements for phasing out assistance to existing eligible areas and the subsequent 'safety net' mechanism, were clear concessions to national government pressure. Negotiated additionality held out the promise for improved monitoring of a principle relegated in importance due to EMU. The Commission's proposals on partnership responded to the mixed experience of different partners across and within Member States. From the perspective of both efficiency and equity, the Commission had good arguments for both deepening and broadening partnerships. Whether national governments would accept these arguments in principle and implement a resulting agreement in practice remained an issue for future observation.

7 |

Multi-Level Governance or
Flexible Gatekeeping?

Introduction

This chapter analyses the utility of approaches discussed in Chapter 1 for explaining developments in EC regional policy. It has five sections. The first section summarizes the analysis of developments in regional policy up to 1993, followed by analysis of policy implementation. The second section considers the competing explanations of structural policy provided by multi-level governance and liberal intergovernmentalism. Section 3 refers to the framework of 'areas of explanation' set out in Chapter 1, and discusses how multi-level governance and liberal intergovernmentalism deal with each of these areas. The utility of the policy networks approach is discussed in Section 4. The chapter concludes by proposing the arguments of *flexible gatekeeping*, to be used as a counterpoint to the arguments of multi-level governance in future sectoral studies.

1. EU-Level Developments in Regional Policy

Creating Regional Policy

For conceptual purposes, Chapter 1 distinguished between levels of explanation *above* (*or external to*), *within* (or internal to) and *below* (*'domestic' politics*) the EU system. While again emphasizing that, in reality, the distinction between these levels of explanation are blurred and that understanding the linkages between them is crucially important, this distinction nevertheless provides a useful starting point for explaining developments in regional policy.

Chapter 2 concluded that a number of factors within, below and above the EC political system contributed to the creation of regional policy. *Within* the EC system, two factors were particularly important:

enlargement of the Community and the political imperatives of economic and monetary union. Not only were decisions on these developments essentially intergovernmental, but all the major decisions on the creation of regional policy were taken by the Council of Ministers. National governments collectively controlled the financial resources needed for establishing a regional fund and controlled the political resources provided by the pivotal role of the Council in the Community decision-making process. In contrast, the Commission's influence was limited to the argument that its stock of technical expertise and informational resources meant it was uniquely placed to assess the needs of EC regions and respond according to Community-wide criteria.

Despite the limited resources available to the Commission, particularly its dependence on national governments for support in the Council, the Commission played a key role in keeping the regional policy issue alive throughout the 1960s and 1970s when many factors appeared to conspire against it. That a Community regional policy of any kind emerged by 1975 owed no small part to Commission persistence, and particularly that of DG XVI. The continual 'prodding' of the Council and 'forging of coalitions' undertaken by the Commission appears more significant in retrospect than contemporary authors suggested. In this period, the Commission—and, to a lesser extent, the European Parliament and other allies—laid the foundations for more significant developments in regional policy after 1975.

The importance of *external* events in shaping regional policy was well illustrated by the outbreak of the Yom Kippur War and the subsequent oil crisis. In particular, this challenged assumptions about continued economic growth and also hardened the German negotiating position against the potentially oil-rich UK over its regional policy demands. The tone of regional policy negotiations changed and there is evidence to suggest the Yom Kippur War encouraged the tendency towards a regional policy characterized by an intergovernmental 'carve-up' rather than one based on objective Community indicators.

The importance of *domestic politics* to regional policy negotiations was illustrated by the different positions taken by the UK government over the creation of a regional fund over time. The Euro-enthusiastic Conservative government was replaced by a Euro-sceptic Labour government in 1974, bringing contrasting UK priorities to EC negotiations that reduced the salience of a deal on regional policy. Ultimately the UK position was shaped by the political imperative of retaining national control over both the public expenditure implications and distributive impact of EC regional policy in the UK; a Treasury view.

Regional Policy 1975–1988

As the creation of regional policy was shaped primarily by inter-governmental bargains, so was its early development. While most early accounts attached some significance to the Commission's role, and to a lesser extent that of the European Parliament, national governments were seen to dominate an EC-level process restricted largely to institu-tional actors, with little scope for the direct involvement of non-gov-ernmental or subnational interests. And, while the conceptualization of the creation and early development of regional policy as a straight-forward Commission–Council dialogue was challenged, this dialogue remained at the centre of decision-making.

Where the Commission made progress over its regional policy aspirations before 1988, it did so through its agenda-setting powers. The Commission's *formal* right to propose policies and this, in addition to its informal characteristics of 'expertise, brokering skills and institu-tional persistence' makes the Commission particularly well placed to set the 'substantive agenda for the decisions taken by member states' (Pollack 1996: 449). This combination of formal and informal resources allows the Commission to act as a *policy entrepreneur*, set-ting the agenda 'by identifying policy problems, proposing and "selling" policy proposals, and brokering compromises among the member states on the terms of the policies ultimately adopted' (Pollack 1996: 449). Thus, while national governments rejected and diluted many of the Commission's proposals for regional policy from the 1960s through to the early 1980s, it was significant that these were Commission proposals and some were adopted: the non-quota system and programme contracts were notable examples. In particular, the Commission had resources of expertise and information to prepare solid arguments for these proposals, and secured sufficient support from national governments dependent on the Commission for these resources. As Pollack noted, 'Commission influence is greatest where information is imperfect, uncertainty about future developments is high, and/or asymmetrical distribution of information between the Commission and the member states favours the former' (1996: 449).

In the period up to 1988, the Commission made piecemeal progress rather than great leaps forward. However, the Commission depended on sufficient national governments accepting its arguments, which in many instances did not happen. Additionality was an important example of this and the Commission's failure to make progress on this key principle was an illustration of the Council's resilience on matters of 'high policy' to national governments. However, while the reforms of 1979 and 1984 failed to convert ERDF from a system of reimbursement to an effective instrument of regional policy, they contained the seeds for future policy development seen in the 1988 reform.

The 1988 Reform
By the time of the 1988 reform, there was general agreement among academic commentators that national governments dominated the EC regional policy process. The consensus was such that, in 1992, McAleavey's work on regional policy was developed in response to 'previous accounts of the regional policy process in the Community as a virtual paragon of intergovernmentalism' (1992: 3). It was in the period after 1988 that intergovernmental interpretations were seriously challenged.

In terms of the budgetary envelope agreed in 1988, a relatively straightforward intergovernmentalist interpretation explained the agreement. The more prosperous Member States strongly supported the completion of the single market and wanted this market extending to include Spain and Portugal. In this context, the doubling of the structural funds was accepted by the likely paymaster governments as the trade-off for securing general agreement on issues of greater importance to them. Advocates of multi-level governance did not contest this interpretation. However, interpretations over other aspects of the reform were contested. A good example was the partnership principle, which involved the mobilization of subnational actors. This was seen as a Commission initiative, consistent with previous Commission attempts to increase the involvement of subnational actors in structural policy-making.

Again, the context for Commission progress on partnership and other aspects of the reform was set by national governments through intergovernmental bargains over the single market programme and enlargement. In a context of these integrationist moves and a general economic optimism, Commission proposals were more readily accepted by national governments than previously.

If the outcome of the negotiations over the 1988 reform of the struc-

tural fund was shaped decisively by asymmetries in the relative intensity of national preferences across related policy sectors, the bargaining
space these asymmetries provided also allowed the Commission to
make significant advances over regional policy. It did so because the
prior intergovernmental bargains that shaped the context in which the
reform took place provided the Commission with important resources
of political legitimacy. Moreover, the Commission had built up significant informational resources that strengthened its ability to set the
agenda and thus influence the outcome of the negotiations considerably. However, securing changes in the regulations was one thing;
effective implementation could not be assumed.

The 1993 Reform

If the 1988 reform of the structural funds suggested the Commission
had advanced its influence over regional policy-making, the detail of
the 1993 reform was confirmation this advance had been halted and the
Commission was facing retreat. As with 1988, prior intergovernmental
bargains set the context for 1993 reform. By 1993, however, the political resources afforded by previous decisions were in the possession of
national governments seeking to secure escape routes from the
demands of an increasingly supranational policy sector. The exchanges
over additionality were strong evidence of this. In the context of the
convergence criteria for monetary union agreed at Maastricht, the
Commission was unable to pursue genuine additionality: while additionality required Member States to demonstrate additional public
expenditure, the convergence criteria put a squeeze on domestic public
spending.

   Other changes reflected the reassertion of national government preferences. For example, while the partnership principle was confirmed,
national government remained in control of the designation of
'appropriate partners'. In addition, a new clause stated that the choice
of partners should be consistent with 'the framework of each member
state's national rules and current practices'. This meant that, where
Member States took a narrow definition of the relevant partners, this
would be acceptable if consistent with national rules and current practices. However, the inclusion of the Community Economic Development (CED) priority in some UK structural fund programmes was a
Commission-inspired initiative that promised to broaden the range of
partners to include local community representatives.

The creation of the management committee to oversee Community Initiatives (CIs) created a degree of national government involvement that would curtail Commission discretion. In the conflict over the implementation of additionality after 1988, the Commission had used its control over the content, coverage and timing of CIs to undermine UK government arguments. The 1993 changes meant this would be less possible in future. Finally, the creation of the Cohesion Fund in 1993 was a direct response to the demands of the governments of poorer Member States and provided little scope in its administrative arrangements for the innovations of structural policy.

In summary, the 1993 reform provided a measure of how the relative influence of actors at EU level can fluctuate within a policy sector over a short period of time. The context of regional policy reform changed dramatically in the five years after the 1988. This led to a shift in the balance of political resources away from the Commission to the Council at the EU level, which was reflected in the 1993 outcome. As the context for EU regional policy-making changed, the Commission's attempt at a great leap forward in 1988 was soon followed by several paces back in 1993.

The changeable context of EU regional policy decisions made it difficult to generalize about the power of the various actors involved. Hindsight tells that claims made after the 1988 reform that the Commission had established itself at the centre of the regional policy process were overstated. However, this should lead to caution in declaring that the 1993 reform provided definitive evidence of the claims of intergovernmentalism. While the history of EU-level regional policy-making demonstrated the underlying resilience of national governments, the regional policy process was still relatively new and fluid. This being so, fluctuations in the influence of different actors were a prominent feature. Existing actors continued to test the boundaries of their powers in this emerging political arena and the greater involvement of new actors added a new and largely untested dimension. The European Parliament acquired new powers over regional policy in the early 1990s and the significance of these powers had yet to unfold. The emergence of transnational networks such as EURACOM, which played an influential role in lobbying for and shaping the RECHAR programme, added a further dimension to EU-level decision-making which made predictions for the future less certain. At domestic level, the proliferation of new actors started the process of shifting resources away from subnational government in some Member States, but it remained uncertain whether this process of fragmentation would pose a lasting challenge to the dominant role of national governments. As Marks put it:

> The story of 1988 through 1993 reveals the potential for ongoing institutional redesign in cohesion policy as a spillover from intergovernmental bargains in other EU areas, as a result of mobilization of new actors, particularly subnational actors, and in response to shifting preferences of subnational, national and supranational actors. To describe cohesion policy over the past several years...is to describe a moving target'(Marks 1996a: 420).

The 1999 Reform

The Commission's proposals for the 1999 reform of the structural funds implied an ongoing renationalization in some areas, but also attempted to strengthen some existing policy principles. These included an attempt at greater concentration, which was accepted by national governments in principle, but would face strong challenges from Member States likely to be most affected. By mid-1998, concessions had already been made to national government demands for a transitional period of funding and a 'safety net' to protect those areas already eligible. Further, national governments looked set to play a stronger role over eligibility for Objective 2 areas as well as attempting to maintain control over Objective 1 allocations.

Aspects of simplification in the Commission's proposals were a direct response to domestic criticism of overly bureaucratic procedures. However, simplification was seen by some as an opportunity also for national governments to reduce Commission involvement. That the Commission would be reducing its involvement in partnership activities appeared to confirm this trend. For its part, the Commission believed it could maintain a strong role within monitoring committees and by developing more effective monitoring and implementation procedures.

The principle of programming would be maintained, but reduced to two stages from three for all but the largest programmes. This was generally welcomed as a way of streamlining the process. Community Initiatives were reduced in number from thirteen to three. Again, this was generally welcomed by national governments, yet the Commission believed CIs would continue to provide scope for it to experiment and innovate. Finally, negotiated additionality promised improved monitoring of a principle that was largely redefined to the benefit of national governments in the context of attempts to meet monetary union convergence criteria.

If much of the reform proposals suggested renationalization, remained an important exception. The partnership model was accepted in principle across Member States, but the interpretation and implementation of partnership had varied tremendously. In 1998, the Commission proposed a tighter definition of its partnership requirements, and, from the perspectives of both efficiency and equity, it had good arguments for both deepening and broadening partnerships. However, whether national governments would accept these arguments in principle and interpret and implement any agreement in accordance with Commission wishes remained an issue for future observation.

The Importance of Implementation

The introduction of the partnership principle was arguably the most significant political development in regional policy after its creation in 1975. While predicated on the argument that partnerships would improve policy effectiveness, the partnership principle challenged established hierarchical relationships between central and subnational governments. Despite this, relations within structural fund partnerships were often asymmetrical. In particular, structural fund regulations gave central government a high degree of control over the key political and financial resources within partnerships. Other actors were able to mobilize political, financial and informational resources to different degrees in different Member States and even within Member States. The outcome was that, while structural fund partnerships challenged existing territorial relations within Member States, this challenge was met with different degrees of resistance and with different outcomes. In some Member States, subnational actors were mobilized, but not necessarily empowered. In others, the impact on territorial relations was more significant.

The 1988 reform of the structural funds provided a classic illustration of how EU-level agreements could be frustrated at the policy implementation stage. The principles of partnership and additionality were implemented very differently by Member States in practice. Importantly, implementation of the principles of additionality and partnership showed that, where national governments were determined to resist unwanted domestic outcomes from developments at EU level, they are able to play a 'gatekeeper' role throughout the policy process to the realization of policy outcomes. This suggested that existing explanations of the EU policy process would be strengthened by analysing the impact of implementation on *outcomes*. Thus, where the gatekeeper notion was useful in describing the behaviour of national governments in EU policy-making, it made sense to refer to an *extended gatekeeper* operating at different stages of the policy process, including implementation.

A Way Forward?

In his study of ERDF implementation in western Scotland, McAleavey (1995a: 20) conceptualized policy implementation as a process of informal *contracting*: an 'agreement among actors who recognize their mutual interests and agree to modify their behaviour in ways that are mutually beneficial' (Majone 1994: 13). However, this form of contracting is incomplete because it is unlikely that partners would be able to 'foresee and accurately describe all the relevant contingencies that might arise in the course of the contract, and that they be willing and able to agree upon an efficient course of action for each possible contingency' (Majone 1994, quoted in McAleavey 1995a: 21).

McAleavey described how interviewees emphasized the importance of the 'human dimension' in the effective implementation of programmes. In terms of social science, this could be conceptualized 'not just in the technocratic sense of promoting expertise, but also as the evolution of *reputation* effects and *trust*' (1995a: 338; emphasis original). The development of trust between partners involved in structural policy 'makes it unnecessary to resort to excessive formalization and detailed specification of the rules of exchange', and 'therefore makes the entire process of political exchange potentially more elastic, dynamic and wider' (Mutti 1990: 210). In this context, the development of trust between partners is crucial to the effective implementation of policy. As such, the model of *incomplete contracting* may provide a valuable additional tool for highlighting the political aspects of policy implementation generally and the importance of trust to effective policy implementation specifically. As McAleavey (1995a: 345) put it:

> Complete contracts, totally pre-programmed in all respects are simply
> not a feasible model for EC legislation...The wider potential value of
> the incomplete contracting model is that it could take analysis of Com-

munity policy-making beyond a primarily legal perspective to incorporate the significance of trust between contracting partners.

The development of trust between partners for the effective implementation of regional policy may be of obvious importance; how it can
be engendered is less obvious. McAleavey (1995a: 339) pointed to
three indirect, but interrelated, ways in which the Commission could
seek to develop trust in structural fund partnerships: 'through the assur-
ance of continuity over time; by supporting the political independence
of key implementing bodies; and through the promotion of professional
networking schemes'. In a study of the EU's URBAN programmes,
Bache (1997) made a number of recommendations for improving partnership working. These included: each partner making clear how they
were elected or selected; what their lines of organizational
accountability were; and what they intended to contribute to the partnership. In addition, the report called for training to be made available
to new and existing partners on both partnership working and structural
fund processes. Finally, it was suggested there be greater flexibility in
the match-funding requirements to reduce the financial (and therefore
political) dependence of smaller organizations on larger ones generally,
and of community actors on local institutions specifically (Bache
1997).

Multi-Level Governance and
(Liberal) Intergovernmentalism Assessed

In a study of structural policy-making, Gary Marks suggested that a
weakness in the traditional conceptualizations of EU policy-making,
namely intergovernmentalism and neofunctionalism, was that they
missed a 'crucial element in the whole picture, namely, the increasing
importance of subnational levels of decision-making and their myriad
connections with other levels' (Marks 1993: 392). Moreover, Marks
(1993) suggested that the 1988 reform of the structural funds and the
RECHAR dispute were both strong evidence of what he described as the
emergence of 'multi-level governance'. The institutional reforms of
1988 were drawn up by the Commission and approved by Member
States with only minor revisions (Marks 1993: 399-401), while the
RECHAR dispute confirmed the claim that 'structural policy has provided subnational governments and the Commission with new political

resources and opportunities in an emerging multilevel policy arena' (Marks 1993: 403).

While Marks's assessment of the RECHAR dispute was not inaccurate, it failed to consider the implementation of the agreement reached between the Commission and the UK government. While the 1988 reform provided the Commission and subnational authorities with new political resources and opportunities, this did not necessarily detract from the ability of national governments to determine policy outcomes. The importance of these new political resources and opportunities could be understood most fully once policy decisions had been implemented: analysis of the implementation of additionality and partnership illustrated the limitations of Commission and subnational authorities' powers when faced by a determined national government gatekeeper.

Pollack's response to Marks was essentially, though, as he put it, not 'mindlessly', intergovernmental. Central to his argument was the point that 'Member states…establish the institutional context within which both the Commission and regional governments act, and it is within this intergovernmental context that the precise roles and influence of supranational and subnational actors can best be specified' (1995: 362).

Pollack, following Moravcsik, stated that the context of the 1988 reform was favourable for the exercise of Commission authority as Member State preferences 'converged around a radical reform of the Funds which had been rejected by key member states, such as the UK, in previous reform negotiations' (1995: 372). Despite this, Pollack's reformulation of intergovernmentalism acknowledged that the Commission's agenda-setting powers were important in securing agreements on Community Initiatives (1995: 375) and implementation arrangements (1995: 385), notably the partnership requirements, which shaped part of the institutional framework after 1988. However, along the same lines as Moravcsik, Pollack suggested the power of the Commission that allowed it to secure these agreements was given by national governments and could also be taken away at their discretion. This provides the basis of his explanation for the outcome of the 1993 reform negotiations that were characterized by a swing back to national control over EC regional policy-making.

While it has been acknowledged here that the Commission had a favourable context within which to advance its regional policy ambitions in 1988 due to prior intergovernmental decisions, the argument presented here diverges with Pollack's (1995) suggestion that the power available to the Commission is tightly constrained by national governments. Rather, the development of regional policy has shown the Commission's ability to react pragmatically to the context in which regional policy negotiations take place. By doing so, the Commission made significant progress on its regional policy aspirations when circumstances were favourable. Under less favourable circumstances, the Commission presented less ambitious proposals which remained consistent with its long-term objectives. Even in the least favourable context, the Commission had scope for influence within the 'bargaining space' provided by the diverging interests of national governments. The main source of Commission influence was its agenda-setting power derived from both formal and informal resources.

Through its close involvement with regional policy before, but particularly after, 1975, the Commission accumulated informational resources independently of decisions taken by national governments. These resources enhanced its ability to set the agenda and, in practice, this influence could not easily be neutralized by the Council of Ministers. The Council was locked into a relationship of interdependence with the Commission, and, while this relationship was in most instances asymmetrical in favour of the Council, it was characterized by the Commission's ability to use its informational resources to set the agenda in conducive circumstances, as Pollack (1996; see above) noted later. Through these resources the Commission was able to advance regional policy objectives that conflicted with those of at least some national governments.

While the general argument made by Pollack about the importance of national governments over regional policy is not disputed, there was perhaps an initial overemphasis on the degree of completeness with which national governments controlled the policy process. This emphasis softens later in the argument, however, when he states:

> The Commission and the regions are indeed *independent* actors, but they are actors in a play written *essentially* by the member states, and their ability to influence policy outcomes has been circumscribed by the institutional structures established, and periodically revised in light of experience by member states (1995: 385; my emphasis).

The description of the Commission as an 'independent' actor in a play written 'essentially' by Member States contrasts with the earlier and firmer statement that Member States 'establish the institutional context within which both the Commission and regional governments act'. This is a subtle difference, but at least hints that, if national governments are the authors of the play in which other institutions act, the Commission may be making a contribution not readily listed by intergovernmental-ists on the authorship credits. It is more accurate to suggest that the Commission has some independence over regional policy-making through its agenda-setting powers—and this includes influence over the institutional context—and that the 'play' in which the Commission acts is co-authored. However, the evidence at this stage suggests that, for now at least, national governments contribute the bulk of the EU level 'script'. Despite concerns that Pollack understates the independent re-sources available to the Commission, his conclusions about the under-lying resilience of national governments have validity. Yet this resilience is not always most evident at the EU level of policy-making, but during policy implementation.

Intergovernmentalism and Implementation
In his restatement of intergovernmentalism, Pollack acknowledged the importance of implementation, suggesting that 'the analysis of both EC structural policymaking and the implementation of the Structural Funds should begin—but not necessarily end—with an intergovernmental analysis of the preferences of and bargaining among member govern-ments' (1995: 352; my emphasis).

Yet, in Pollack's discussion of *Implementing the 1988 Reforms* (1995: 373-78), his analysis was not of the implementation process, but of the conditions under which implementation takes place. Thus, Pollack treated the RECHAR dispute as a study in implementation when in fact it was about *how* the programme would be implemented. The end of the RECHAR dispute was not the end of the policy process, but signalled the beginning of the policy implementation stage proper. As noted above, until the dispute ended, no funds had been released to the UK. An evaluation of the full significance of the RECHAR dispute could only be made once funds were released and their additionality assessed.

In taking the end of the RECHAR dispute as the end of the implemen-tation story, Pollack accepted the dispute as the 'prototypical case' cited by Marks and others for the argument that the 1988 reforms would have the 'unintended consequences' of empowering the Com-mission and mobilizing subnational governments, with the possibility of 'outflanking' member governments (Pollack 1995: 374). Pollack dealt with the anomaly of the RECHAR dispute within his framework by describing it as 'an unusually public and confrontational example of both Commission and regional influence' (Pollack 1995. 374), citing the Commission's use of its greater agenda-setting power over CIs as important. Yet analysis of policy implementation after the RECHAR dispute strengthened the intergovernmentalist argument in this case and undermined the multi-level governance claim that 'in the implementation phase between two reviews state actors play a much less predominant role' (Hooghe 1996a: 16). Despite the Commission's greater agenda-setting power over CIs and the mobilization of UK local authorities in support of the Commission, there was little evidence to suggest these factors had a significant impact on the policy outcome of the RECHAR dispute. In short, the extended gatekeeper role was effective at the implementation stage.

Also in the discussion of 'implementation', Pollack made the point that 'Collectively, the Council has adopted fund regulations which, despite the principles of partnership and additionality, maintain much of the gatekeeping ability of the member governments' (1995: 376); and that 'for the 90 percent of the Structural Funds allocated to national and regional CSFs, the member governments remain the gatekeepers to regional participation in Community structural policymaking' (1995: 377). The evidence presented here does not dispute these points. However, the statements refer to EU-level agreements shaping the conditions for implementation and are not derived from an analysis of the implementation process itself. If we are interested in assessing the effectiveness of national governments as gatekeepers, we should assess this role throughout the policy process. This being so, the evidence of this research suggests there is much validity in Pollack's argument that 'The level of success or failure of each member government in maintaining its gatekeeper role seems to be largely a function of the pre-existing distribution of power among the central government and sub-national governments in each member state' (1995: 377). Thus it would appear necessary to evaluate the gatekeeper role throughout the policy process on a case-by-case basis to provide the fullest understanding of the role played by national governments in structural policy-making.

Theoretical Convergence?

There appears a tendency in the recent attempts to theorize regional policy-making to emphasize differences in theoretical positions that are more apparent than real: an attempt to put clear water between competing theories when the water is muddied and the theories as complementary as they are conflicting. The recent debate surrounding EU regional policy-making was between those on one side who explained the process as essentially intergovernmental (Moravcsik, Pollack) and those who suggested the emergence of multi-level governance (Marks, Hooghe). The problem for intergovernmentalists was in accounting for the role played by other actors in the process, notably the Commission, without undermining their key proposition that national governments dominate the process. The problems for multi-level governance theorists was in justifying the importance of 'other actors', particularly subnational governments, while acknowledging that national governments remain the major players in the process. In reality, the two came closer together on this issue as they attempted to account for a policy process where the influence of various actors fluctuated considerably over a short period of time and at different stages of the policy process. In the rapidly changing political environment of the European Union, where the relative influence of existing actors is not settled and where new actors are entering the process at an accelerating rate, it has proved difficult to sustain the arguments of these general theories in relation to EC regional policy-making.

In terms of EU-level decision-making over regional policy, the debate moved from one concerned with fundamental questions of power between the respective actors to one of emphasis. National governments were seen to be dominant: the central issue was one of how complete and how lasting this dominance is. On the one hand, the evidence presented here suggests the description of the EU regional policy process as 'essentially intergovernmental' has some merit. However, this description fails to capture the complexities of the relationships involved in a dynamic policy process. There would appear to be a case for a shift away from broad explanations of EU policy-making. The policy process is not only different across EU policy sectors, but also across issues within the same sector and has different characteristics at different stages and over relatively short time-periods.

Areas of Explanation

The framework presented in Chapter 1 provided five areas of explanation for understanding the politics of EU regional policy: the question of *who decides what and to what effect*. The following section discusses how multi-level governance and liberal intergovernmentalism deal with each of these areas of explanation.

1. Factors 'above' or 'external' to the EU System
Both neofunctionalism and intergovernmentalism acknowledged the influence of factors external to the EU system over internal developments, but did not develop this to any great extent. This factor remains relatively underdeveloped in the more recent conceptualizations of multi-level governance and liberal intergovernmentalism. Multi-level governance focuses on the constraints on national government autonomy from other actors operating 'within' the EU system, notably the Commission and subnational authorities. The focus of liberal intergovernmentalism is also primarily on processes internal to the EU system, arguing that 'international agreement requires that the interests of dominant domestic groups in different countries converge' (Moravcsik 1993: 487). However, as Caporaso and Keeler (1995: 44) put it,

> these preferences are themselves theoretically unexplained. Once interests are given, the negotiating history is supportive of the intergovernmental model. But taking interests as given is a powerful move that allows realism (modified to be sure) to claim much theoretical ground.

Here, more could be said in particular on how the international context may influence the convergence of Member State preferences. Sandholtz and Zysman (1989: 96) provided insight at this level of analysis by suggesting that 'structural change was a necessary, though not a sufficient condition for the renewal of the European project'. More emphasis on the relationship between changes in the international economy and the convergence of Member State preferences would strengthen the liberal intergovernmentalist framework in particular.

2. Factors 'below' the EU System: Domestic Politics
Moravcsik acknowledged the impact of domestic politics on national positions at EU-level negotiations. He argued that 'the foreign policy goals of national governments are viewed as varying in response to shifting pressure from domestic social groups, whose preferences are aggregated through political institutions' (1993: 481). In different circumstances, national governments have greater or less autonomy to decide policy goals because 'at times the principal–agent relationship between social pressures and state policies is tight; at times, "agency

slack" in the relationship permits rational governments to exercise greater discretion' (1993: 484). Here, more could be said about why interest groups are sometimes important and sometimes not, or why some groups regularly have more success in persuading governments than others. In particular, the approach could theorize how social and political structures provide more resources to some interests rather than others which allow them greater influence over governments.

Multi-level governance does not dispute the influence of 'domestic' politics on EU policy-making. However, it takes issue with traditional intergovernmental claims that national governments monopolize the aggregation of domestic interests. While this criticism is addressed by Moravcsik's conceptualization of *liberal* intergovernmentalism, multi-level governance places greater emphasis on the penetration of domestic polities. This is the argument that 'political arenas are interconnected rather than nested…The clear separation between domestic and international politics, which is assumed in the state-centric model, is blurred under multi-level governance' (Marks, Hooghe and Blank 1996: 346).

3. Factors 'within' or 'internal to' the EU System:
Levels of Decision-Making and Issue Linkage

In Chapter 1, it was argued that, in practical terms, different stages of the policy process are interconnected. For analytical purposes, however, it is useful to make a distinction between EU-level decision-making and policy implementation, which is in practice largely a matter for Member States. Further subdivision of these two broad policy-making levels is also helpful. At EU level, distinct policy-making stages can be identified. Also, some commentators identify a hierarchy of policy decisions across sectors which help to explain *issue linkage*. Subdivisions within regional policy implementation can be made at four stages of 'structural programming' (see below).

At EU level, there is a consensus among commentators that EU-level agreements over regional policy are linked to decisions in other policy areas. Of particular importance historically have been moves to complete economic and monetary union and the enlargement of the Community. Moravcsik (1993) and others refer to bargains over regional policy as 'side-payments' by richer Member States to poorer Member States for their cooperation in policy areas where more affluent Member States have a greater intensity of preference. In the policy networks tradition, Peterson (1995a) made a similar distinction between levels of analysis. This distinction would conceptualize the 1988 reform agree ments, for example, as 'policy-setting decisions' taken at the *systemic* level, which relate to the *super-systemic* decisions to launch the completion of the internal market by 1992 and the enlargement of the EC to include Portugal and Spain. In both cases, previous decisions provided implicit and explicit agreements to reform regional policy in a substantive way, broadly shaping the 'rules of the game' under which bargaining took place. Thus the eventual agreement reached in 1988 was an illustration not only of the interdependence of Member States in the EU but also of issue linkage between policy decisions across sectors.

In assessing the influence of national, subnational and supranational actors over EU structural policy, Marks (1996) argued the need to disaggregate the component parts of the policy process in addition to accounting for spatial variations. Three distinct phases were identified: bargaining the financial envelope, creating the institutional context, and structural programming. The first concerns decisions over financial redistribution; the second concerns how funds should be administered, the 'institutional context'; and the third is concerned with the operationalization of CSFs (Marks 1996: 389-406).

Supranational versus National Policy Control. At the centre of the traditional debate between IR realists and pluralists was the influence of the Commission. This remained central to the debate between liberal intergovernmentalism and multi-level governance. There was agreement between commentators that the broad framework for regional policy reforms is largely established by national governments, particularly in relation to the budgetary envelope. Yet, while there is agreement that the broad context for regional policy reform is generally set by previous Council decisions on other issues, the extent to which national governments shape the detail of the reform, including the institutional arrangements, is contested. Hooghe (1996: 97) argued:

> the side-payment is only the first step in a multi-stage process. Once the financial envelope is decided, the Commission draws up the regulatory blueprint of the policies for spending the money. It does that by virtue of its monopoly of initiative.

Moravcsik argued that the Commission's influence is a cost of cooperation to member governments, which is judged to be less than the benefits. This argument assigns a precision to the process of international cooperation that is difficult to justify. The 'costs' to national governments are as difficult to calculate as are the benefits to governments from international cooperation in the form of the EU. Within the emerging political framework of the European Union, the Commission's agenda-setting powers distinguish it as an institution that is constitutionally complementary to the Council of Ministers, but at times politically in conflict.

Moravcsik's argument that the Commission's agenda-setting power is limited 'by the Council's previous delegation and ultimate decision' (1993: 513) is stronger in theory than in practice. While the 'Council's previous delegations' are a starting point for understanding the Commission's influence, the constraint of 'ultimate decision' is not straightforward—particularly when the Commission has constructed alliances with national governments. The Commission can and does act in ways not foreseen by national governments. Commission *activity* over the RECHAR programme was a good example, even if the policy outcome was commonly misinterpreted. National governments are locked into a complex system of international agreements and political relationships in which the Commission is deeply enmeshed. The Commission has accumulated significant informational, financial and political resources which have not always been mobilized in the interests of national governments per se.

While the Commission was an important actor in the 1988 reform negotiations, the history of regional policy hitherto had been characterized by fluctuations in the power of the actors involved. Previously, there had been moments when the Commission had advanced its policy agenda, but usually national governments had proven resilient in determining important policy outcomes. This history should have pointed to caution in making claims about the irresistible rise of Commission power as a consequence of the outcome of the 1988 reform. While 1988 undoubtedly marked a high point in the Commission's achievements in regional policy negotiations, much of this achievement was due to factors external to the Commission. It is evident that the Commission exploited fully its agenda-setting powers, but it is also evident the Commission was given considerable scope for exercising these powers through prior agreements in other policy areas. While the Commission illustrated that it was willing and able to act when the opportunity arose, this opportunity was presented by a particular set of circumstances. In short, the context was crucial, and there were no guarantees that the context would be so favourable next time around. Unfortunately for the Commission, it was not.

4. Policy Implementation

Marks acknowledges implementation as an important stage in the policy process. Moreover, in terms of 'structural programming', he provides a helpful subdivision of the implementation stages. While implementation was not a key part of Moravcsik's work, this theme was included in an 'essentially' intergovernmental position by Pollack. However, as argued above, the treatment of implementation by both Marks and Pollack is not as full as it could be.

5. The Role of 'Non-State' Actors

Traditional intergovernmentalism placed little emphasis on the role of 'non-state' actors, whereas liberal intergovernmentalism acknowledges pluralism in domestic foreign policy formation. Neofunctionalism highlighted the role of 'interests' in furthering European integration, while multi-level governance emphasized the increasing importance of subnational actors in policy-making.

Areas of Explanation: Conclusion

If the major strength of liberal intergovernmentalism for explaining regional policy-making is its emphasis on the continuing resilience of national governments, this approach would be strengthened by the addition of a *theory* of the convergence of national government preferences; by strengthening the theory of 'domestic' foreign policy formation; and also from greater emphasis on the gatekeeper role of national governments at the implementation stage. Accommodating the independent role of the Commission over EU-level regional policy decisions appears increasingly difficult within the liberal intergovernmentalist framework, although Pollack contributed to this.

The multi-level governance approach has a number of strengths. It places greater emphasis than intergovernmentalism on disaggregating the state, has greater focus on decision-making at a number of levels, and argues that the influence of different actors fluctuates across and within policy sectors. In terms of regional policy, however, it has a tendency to overstate the importance of subnational actors and, related to this, a need to focus more on implementation through to policy outcomes where national government preferences may be revealed as most significant. This point is particularly important because proponents of the multi-level governance model suggest it is most prevalent at the policy implementation stage.

Assessing the Policy Networks Approach

While not the most important aspect of the policy networks approach, the *typology* of the Rhodes model contributes to the understanding of the various formal and informal channels through which EU regional policy is implemented. For example, regional structural fund partnerships closely fitted the 'policy community' typology and what developed during the RECHAR dispute resembled an 'issue network' which included a larger number of participants with a more limited degree of interdependence. In 1986, Rhodes described the 'UK ERDF network' as an issue network, but subsequent developments demand a revision of this. While, in the 1980s and early 1990s, the main national and regional ERDF networks were essentially *intergovernmental* (in the terminology of the Rhodes model), by the mid-1990s this had changed with the increased involvement of non-governmental actors in the regional policy process. At regional level, non-governmental actors were already well represented on programme monitoring committees. There is now a series of complex overlapping networks within and across Member States. As noted above, these networks have different characteristics which cover the extremes on the typology continuum provided by Rhodes, from policy communities to issue networks.

If the initial value of the policy networks approach was in mapping out actors involved and ordering information, more substantive value was provided by the concept of *power dependence*. This allowed for a greater understanding of the relative influence over policy outcomes at the implementation stage and deserves greater prominence in the policy networks literature. Power dependence facilitates the understanding that power is situational, that 'Power enjoyed on one occasion may not be transferable to other sets of conditions' (Knoke 1990: 2). This would appear to be a particularly important feature of power in the rapidly changing political arena of the European Union.

Rhodes (1997) is explicit about the limitations of the policy networks approach. Here it has been most useful in providing the analytical tools to assess and inform theories of EU decision-making. Despite its explicit limitations, the Rhodes model provides useful tools for understanding the dynamics of structural fund partnerships in particular and evolving characteristics of EC policy-making more generally. As Keohane and Hoffmann (1991: 5) argued, 'the Community political system can best be visualized as an elaborate set of networks, closely linked in some ways, particularly decomposed in others'. Consequently, there is 'a growing convergence among international relations and comparative politics scholars conceptualizing the EU as a multilevel structure of governance where private, governmental, transnational and supranational actors deal with each other in highly complex networks of varying density, as well as horizontal and vertical depth' (Risse-Kappen 1996: 62). Within this emerging reality of complex and overlapping networks, the Rhodes model can assist in answering the question of *who does what and to what effect.*

Multi-Level Governance or Flexible Gatekeeping?

No single theoretical model exists that facilitates analysis of EU policy-making from the EU-level decision-making stages through implementation to policy outcomes. The theories from international relations traditionally applied to EU decision-making, intergovernmentalism and neofunctionalism focused on initial decision-making at the EU level. This can be the equivalent of seeing the tip of an iceberg as the most important part. Decisions taken at EU-level have to be implemented and, within the EU, this is largely the task of national governments in 15 different domestic contexts. Under such circumstances, the potential for transforming the initial policy objectives into very different policy outcomes is obvious. At the very least, there is the likelihood of variations in policy outcomes between Member States once implementation stage bargaining has taken place.

While multi-level governance has considerable merit in describing the emerging polity of the EC, the evidence from regional policy is that national governments operate as gatekeepers at various stages of the policy process to put a brake on the emergence of a truly multi-level system of governance. On occasions, the consequence of national government gatekeeping is a political arena characterized less by multi-level governance than by *multi-level participation*: actors from sub-national and supranational levels participate, but do not significantly influence decision-making outcomes. In short, multi-level governance needs to take greater account of the gatekeeping powers of national governments across all stages of policy-making, over time and across issues. Previous conceptualizations of gatekeeping have focused on EU-level activity; here it is argued that gatekeeping is a *flexible* concept that may be practised by governments at different stages of the policy process. Moreover, the gatekeeping role of governments is flexible over time: the renationalization of aspects of regional policy in 1993 provided evidence of this. Finally, gatekeeping is flexible across issues: while the UK government accepted the bulk of the Commission's 1988 reform proposals, it did not compromise on additionality.

The arguments of *flexible gatekeeping* assume national governments are crucial actors in the EU policy process, but not that an essentially intergovernmental interpretation of decision-making is necessarily accurate on all issues, at all stages of policy-making, or over time. The concept of flexible gatekeeping does, however, suggest that a focus on initial decision-making rather than the whole policy process can lead to an underestimation and thus misrepresentation of the underlying power of national governments able to mobilize considerable resources to shape policy outcomes at the implementation stage. While this may strengthen intergovernmentalist claims and weaken the claims of multi-level governance, the extent to which this is so must be a matter for empirical investigation of different policy sectors; however, this investigation should not begin and end with analysis of EU-level agreements or with an incomplete conceptualization of what constitutes implementation.

Conclusion

At the centre of this discussion has been the question of *who decides what and to what effect* in relation to EC regional policy. It is clear that the answer to the second part of this question is linked to the answer of the first part. The answer to part one of the question is that control over regional policy remains contested and can fluctuate over time, between issues and at different levels of policy-making. The two principle combatants are national governments and the Commission, although other actors have influence to lesser degrees. The history of regional policy has illustrated that an essentially intergovernmentalist interpretation of events has some merit, but fails to capture the complexity of the policy process. In particular, the Commission has advanced objectives of regional policy with political connotations which have met with some success. One connotation has been the increased participation of other actors in the process: partly through negotiating direct transfers of competences from national governments to the Commission itself and partly through encouraging the mobilization of subnational actors within domestic systems and the European arena.

Undoubtedly, regional policy remains a matter of high political (and economic) salience within the European Union. It remains an important expression of European solidarity through the *principle* of transferring resources from stronger regions to weaker regions. It has provided a model of a collaborative approach to economic development; stimulated the creation of new and innovative partnerships at local, regional and national level; and has meant new opportunities for previously excluded governmental and non-governmental actors. Yet understanding the politics of EC regional policy-making and the political *impact* of its outputs remains a complex task. An increasing number of academic approaches have been employed to demystify the politics of EC policy-making including new institutionalism, rational choice theory and theories of regulation. (For an overview, see Caporaso and Keeler 1995; Hix 1994; McAleavey 1995a; and Risse-Kappen 1996.) If there is a consensus in the recent literature, it is not a complete rejection of the international relations debates, but a 'growing dissatisfaction with treating institutional outcomes as lying somewhere on an intergovernmental–supranational continuum' (McAleavey 1995a: 178). This literature confirms the view set out at the very beginning of this book that no single theory can explain the complex politics of policy-making in the European Union. The challenge is to apply the appropriate tools at the appropriate levels of analysis to provide the fullest picture of the politics of EC policy-making. This book provides evidence of how complex the challenge is in providing a complete picture of the politics of a single policy sector.

Bibliography

Anderson, J.J.
    1990   'Skeptical Reflections on a Europe of Regions: Britain, Germany, and the
            ERDF', *Journal of Public Policy* 10.4: 417-47.
    1996   'Germany and the Structural Funds: Unification Leads to Bifurcation', in
            Hooghe (ed.) 1996: 163-94.
Armstrong, H.
    1989   'Community Regional Policy', in J. Lodge (ed.), *The European Com-
            munity and the Challenge of the Future* (London: Pinter Publishers): 167-
            85.
    1993   'Subsidiarity and the Operation of European Community Regional Policy
            in Britain', *Regional Studies* 27.6: 575-606.
    1997   'What Future for Regional Policy?' (PERC Policy Paper, 8; Sheffield:
            Political Economy Research Centre, University of Sheffield).
Bache, I.
    1992   'Bypassing the Centre: Assessing the Value of Local Government Partic-
            ipation in European Community Transgovernmental Coalitions'
            (Dissertation for MA in International Studies, University of Sheffield).
    1995   'Additionality and the Politics of EU Regional Policy Making' (Political
            Economy Working Papers, 2; Sheffield: University of Sheffield).
    1996   'EU Regional Policy: Has the UK Government Succeeded in Playing the
            Gatekeeper Role over the Domestic Impact of the European Regional
            Development Fund?' (Unpublished PhD thesis; Sheffield: University of
            Sheffield).
    1997   'Report on the URBAN Programme for Sheffield (Governance Dimen-
            sion)' (Reproduced in part as a contribution to the interim report for the
            Sheffield URBAN Management Committee by JISER [Joint Initiative on
            Social and Economic Research]; Sheffield: Sheffield Hallam University/
            University of Sheffield, November 1997).
    1998   'Partnerships in Public Policy: Regenerating Sheffield' (Paper presented
            to the conference on Democracy in Europe; Twente, Netherlands:
            University of Twente, 12–14 February 1998).
Bache, I., S. George and R.A.W. Rhodes
    1996   'Cohesion Policy and Subnational Authorities in the UK', in Hooghe
            (ed.) 1996: 294-319.
Bache, I., and D. McGillivray
    1997   'Testing the Extended Gatekeeper: The Law, Practice and Politics of
            Implementing the Drinking Water Directive in the United Kingdom', in

J. Holder (ed.), *The Impact of EC Environmental Law in the United Kingdom* (London: John Wiley): 147-65.

Bachtler, J., and R. Michie
1993 'The Restructuring of Regional Policy in the European Community', *Regional Studies* 27.8: 719-25.
1994 'Strengthening Economic and Social Cohesion? The Revision of the Structural Funds', *Regional Studies* .8: 789-96.

Barrett, S., and C. Fudge (eds.)
1981 *Policy and Action* (London: Methuen).

Barrett, S., and M. Hill
1986 'Policy, Bargaining and Structure in Implementation Theory: Towards an Integrated Perspective', in Goldsmith (ed.) 1986: 34-59.

Beckett, M.
1998 Comments by the UK President of the Board of Trade on the BBC television programme *Newsnight*, 15 March 1998.

Beecham, Cllr J.
1992 'ERDF and Additionality' (Letter to Commissioner Millan from the Chair of the Association of Metropolitan Authorities, 26 October 1992).

Brunskill, I.
1992 'Social Partner Participation in the Operation of the European Structural Funds in the United Kingdom: A Study of Scotland' (Report to the European Commission; Glasgow: University of Strathclyde).

Bulmer, S.
1983 'Domestic Politics and European Policy-Making', *Journal of Common Market Studies* 21.4: 349-63.

Caporaso, J.A., and J.T.S. Keeler
1995 'The European Union and Regional Integration Theory', in Rhodes and Mazey (eds.) 1995: 29-62

Commission (of the European Communities)
1973 'Report on the Regional Problems in the Enlarged Community' (Presented to the Council on 4 May 1973), *Bulletin of the European Communities* 6, Supplement 8/73 (Brussels: European Communities).
1975 Preamble to Regulation (EEC) No. 724/75 of 18 March 1975 establishing a European Regional Development Fund, OJ L73, 21/3/75.
1977 'Guidelines for Community Regional Policy' (Communication and proposal from the Commission to the Council, the Council of Ministers [77] 195 final; Brussels, 7 June 1977).
1985 *Completing the Internal Market* (White Paper from the Commission to the European Council; Milan, 28–29 June 1985; COM [85] 310 final; Brussels: European Communities, 14 June 1985).
1986 *Eleventh Annual Report* (1985) to the Council by the Commission (ERDF the Council of Ministers [86] 545 final; Brussels, 20 October 1986).
1987a *Making a Success of the Single Act: A New Frontier for Europe* (COM [87] final; Brussels: European Communities, 15 February 1987).
1987b 'Europe Without Frontiers: Completing the Internal Market' *European Documentation Periodical* 4/1987 (Luxembourg: Office for Official Publications of the European Communities).

1987c   'Europe without Frontiers: Towards a Large Internal Market', *European File* 17/87 (Luxembourg: Office for Official Publications of the European Communities).

1988   'Provisions for Implementing the Reform of the Structural Funds: Commission Statement on the Council's Common Position' (Communication from the Commission to the Parliament, SEC [88] 1841 final; SYN 151; Brussels: European Communities, 8 December 1988).

1989   *Guide to the Reform of the Community's Structural Funds* (Brussels/Luxembourg: European Communities).

1990   *Annual Report on the Implementation of the Structural Funds* (Luxembourg: Office for Official Publications of the European Communities).

1991   *Annual Report on the Implementation of the Reform of the Structural Funds* (Brussels/Luxembourg: European Communities).

1992   *The ERDF in 1990* (Brussels/Luxembourg: European Communities).

1993a   'The Council's Common Position on the Revision of the Structural Fund Regulations' (Communication from the Commission to the European Parliament, SEC [93] final; SYN 455 SYN 457; Brussels: European Communities, 7 July 1993).

1993b   *Community Structural Funds 1994–99: Revised Regulations and Comments* (Brussels/Luxembourg: European Communities).

1995   *Fifth Annual Report on the Implementation of the Structural Funds, 1993* (COM 95 [30] final; Brussels: European Communities, 20 March 1995).

1996a   *First Report on Economic and Social Cohesion* (Brussels/Luxembourg: European Commission).

1996b   *Social and Economic Inclusion through Regional Development: The Community Economic Development Priority in European Structural Funds in Great Britain* (Brussels: European Commission).

1998a   *Proposed Regulations Governing the Reform of the Structural Funds 2000–2006* (Preliminary version; 18 March 1998, Inforegio).

1998b   'Reform of the Structural Funds' (Explanatory memorandum; http://europa.eu.int/pol/reg/en/info.htm).

Commission DG XVI
1997   'Regional Policy and Cohesion, Newsletter No. 42' (July 1997; http://www.europa.eu.int/en/comm/dg16/news/ennews/en0797.htm).

Council of the European Communities
1993a   'Common Position Adopted by the Council Regarding the Coordination of the Structural Funds' (7609/1/93, REV 1; Brussels, 3 July 1993).

1993b   'Common Position Adopted by the Council Regarding the European Regional Development Fund' (7611/1/93; Brussels, 3 July 1993).

Cram, L.
1997   *Policy Making in the EU: Conceptual Lenses and the Integration Process* (London: Routledge).

CURDS
1997   *Written Evidence to the House of Lords* (Centre for Urban and Regional Development Studies, 1997b): 52-62.

De Witte, B.
    1986   'The Reform of the European Regional Development Fund', *Common Market Law Review* 23: 419-40.
Department of the Environment (DoE)
    1976   'Capital Programmes' (Circular 66/76; London: HMSO).
    1991–95   Circulars to English local authorities on 'Credit Approvals and Annual Capital Guidelines' (London: HMSO).
    1992a   Memo from the Secretary of State (Michael Heseltine) to select cabinet colleagues on inadequacy of existing arrangements for treatment of ERDF receipts in the UK (Leaked to the press on 20 January 1992).
    1992b   'European Regional Development Fund Grants, Credit Approvals for 1992–93: "Other Services" Block' (Letter to local authority chief executives in England from Alan Richardson, Directorate of Planning Services, Department of the Environment, 30 June 1992).
    1992c   ' "Other Services", 1993–94: Forward Indications of Annual Capital Guidelines' (Letter to chief executives in England from Richard Gibson, 11 August 1992).
Dunleavy, P., and R.A.W. Rhodes
    1990   'Core Executive Studies in Britain', *Public Administration* 68: 3-28.
Emerson, M., D. Gros, A. Italianer, J. Pisani-Ferry and H. Reichenbach
    1992   *One Market, One Money: An Evaluation of the Potential Benefits and Costs of Forming an Economic and Monetary Union* (Oxford: Oxford University Press).
European Parliament
    1987a   'Report Drawn up on Behalf of the Temporary Committee for the Success of the Single Act and on the Communication from the Commission of the European Communities Entitled: "Making a Success of the Single Act: A New Frontier for Europe" ' (Session Documents 1987–88, A Series; Document A2-42/87, 4 May 1987).
    1987b   'Opinion of the Committee on Regional Policy and Regional Planning' (Session Documents 1987–88, A Series; Document A2-42/87/Annex, 5 May 1987).
    1987c   'Annex to the Report Drawn up on Behalf of the Temporary Committee for the Success of the Single Act and Opinions on the Communication from the Commission of the European Communities Entitled: "Making a Success of the Single Act: A New Frontier for Europe" ' (Session Documents 1987–88, Series AS; Document A2-42/87/Annex, 8 May 1987).
Eurostat
    1998   Eurostat press release, 18/3/98, http://europa.eu.int/en/comm/eurostat/compres/en/2398/6102398a.htm
George, S.
    1985   *Politics and Policy in the European Community* (Oxford: Clarendon Press).
    1994   'Supranational Actors and Domestic Politics: Integration Theory Reconsidered in the Light of the Single European Act and Maastricht' (Sheffield Papers in International Relations, 22; Sheffield: University of Sheffield).

1996   *Politics and Policy in the European Community* (Oxford: Clarendon Press. 3rd edn).

George, S., and I. Bache
  forthcoming *Politics and Policy in the European Union* (Oxford: Oxford University Press).

Goldsmith, M. (ed.)
  1986   *New Research in Central–Local Relations* (London: Sage).

Haas, E.
  1958   *The Uniting of Europe: Political, Social and Economic Forces 1950–57* (Stanford, CA: Stanford University Press).
  1970   'The Study of Regional Integration: Reflections on the Joy and Anguish of Pretheorizing', *International Organization* 24: 607-46

Hall, R., and D. Van Der Wee
  1992   'Community Regional Policies for the 1990s', *Regional Studies* 26.4: 399-419.

Halstead, J.
  1982   'The Development of the European Regional Fund since 1972' (PhD thesis; Bath: University of Bath).

Heseltine, M. (Secretary of State for the Environment)
  1991   Letter to Secretaries of State for Wales and Scotland regarding inadequacy of existing arrangements for treatment of ERDF receipts in the UK (Leaked to the press on 17 December 1991).

Hix, S.
  1994   'The Study of the European Community: The Challenge to Comparative Politics', *West European Politics* 17.1: 1-30.

Hoffmann, S.
  1964   'The European Process at Atlantic Crosspurposes', *Journal of Common Market Studies* 3 (1964–65): 85-101.
  1966   'Obstinate or Obsolete? The Fate of the Nation State and the Case of Western Europe', *Daedalus* 95: 862-915.
  1982   'Reflections on the Nation-State in Western Europe Today', *Journal of Common Market Studies* 21.1: 21-37.

Hooghe, L.
  1993   'Political-Administrative Adaptation in the EC and Regional Mobilisation: The Politics of the Commission Civil Service under the Structural Funds' (Paper for the Conference on EC Cohesion Policy and National Networks, Centre for European Studies, Nuffield College, 2–5 December 1993).
  1996a   'Introduction: Reconciling EU-Wide Policy and National Diversity', in Hooghe (ed.) 1996: 1-26.
  1996b   'Building a Europe with the Regions: The Changing Role of the European Commission', in Hooghe (ed.) 1996: 89-128.

Hooghe, L. (ed.)
  1996c   *European Integration, Cohesion Policy and Subnational Mobilisation* (Oxford: Oxford University Press).

Hooghe, L., and M. Keating
  1994   'The Politics of European Union Regional Policy', *Journal of European Public Policy* 1.3: 367-93

House of Commons
> 1987   *Select Committee on European Legislation, Fifth Report, Session 1987-88* (London: HMSO).
> 1992   *Hansard*, 17 February 1992 (London: HMSO).
> 1994   *Trade and Industry Committee, Session 1994–95, Regional Policy, Minutes of Evidence, December* (London: HMSO).
> 1995a   *Trade and Industry Committee, Session 1994–95, Fourth Report, Regional Policy* (London: HMSO).
> 1995b   *Trade and Industry Committee, Session 1994–95, Fourth Report, Regional Policy. II. Memoranda of Evidence* (London: HMSO).

House of Lords
> 1981   *Select Committee on the European Communities, Session 1980–81, Fourteenth Report, Regional Policy, with Minutes of Evidence* (London: HMSO).
> 1982   *Select Committee on the European Communities, Session 1981–82, Twelfth Report, Revision of the European Regional Development Fund* (London: HMSO).
> 1988   *Select Committee on the European Communities, Fourteenth Report, 1987–88* (Printed on 17 May; London: HMSO).
> 1991   *Select Committee on the European Communities, Session 1991–92, Fourth Report, EEC Regional Development Policy with Evidence* (London: HMSO).
> 1997a   *Reducing Disparities within the European Union: The Effectiveness of the Structural and Cohesion Funds. I. Report, Select Committee on the European Communities, Session 1996–97, Eleventh Report* (London: The Stationery Office).
> 1997b   *Reducing Disparities within the European Union: The Effectiveness of the Structural and Cohesion Funds. II. Evidence, Select Committee on the European Communities, Session 1996–97, Eleventh Report* (London: The Stationery Office).

Hull, C., and R.A.W. Rhodes
> 1977   *Intergovernmental Relations in the European Community* (Farnborough: Saxon House).

Inforegio News
> 1994   'Structural Funds 1994–99: Allocation of Appropriations: Definitions of Eligible Areas', *DG XVI Newsletter* 1 (EN, February 1994; Brussels: Commission of the European Communities).

Keating, M., and B. Jones (eds.)
> 1985   *Regions in the European Community* (Oxford: Clarendon Press).

Keohane, R., and S. Hoffmann (eds.)
> 1991   *The New European Community: Decisionmaking and Institutional Change* (Boulder, CO: Westview Press).

Kerr, Sir John
> 1992   Letter to Bruce Millan, regarding new UK government arrangements for dealing with the treatment of ERDF grants from the UK Permanent Representative to the EC, 13 February 1992.

Knoke, D.
    1990   *Political Networks: The Structural Perspective* (New York: Cambridge University Press).

Laffan, B.
    1983   'Policy Implementation in the European Community: The European Social Fund as a Case Study', *Journal of Common Market Studies* 21.4: 389-408.
    1992   *Integration and Co-operation in Europe* (London/New York: UACES/ Routledge).

Lilley, P.
    1992   'Statement by the Secretary of State for Trade and Industry on RECHAR', *Hansard*, 17 February 1992.

Lindberg, C.
    1963   *The Political Dynamics of European Economic Integration* (Stanford, CA: Stanford University Press).

Lloyd, P., and R. Megan (with G. Bentley, G. Haughton, T. Hart, J. Peck and J. Shutt)
    1995   'Contested Governance: European Exposure in the English Regions' (Paper presented to the Regional Studies Association Conference, Regional Futures: Past and Present, East and West, Gothenburg, 6–9 May 1995).

Lodge, J. (ed.)
    1993   *The European Community and the Challenge of the Future* (London: Pinter, 2nd edn).

Majone, G.
    1994   'The Development of Social Regulation in the European Community: Policy Externalities, Transaction Costs, Motivational Factors' (Revised version of paper presented at the conference on 'European Integration between Nation and Federation', Hochschule St Gallen, 1–3 September 1994).

Marks, G.
    1992   'Structural Policy in the European Community', in Sbragia (ed.) 1992: 191-224.
    1993   'Structural Policy and Multilevel Governance in the EC', in A. Cafruny and G. Rosenthal (eds.), *The State of the European Community*. II. *The Maastricht Debates and Beyond* (Harlow: Longman): 391-410.
    1996a   'Exploring and Explaining Variation in EU Cohesion Policy', in Hooghe (ed.) 1996: 388-422.
    1996b   'An Actor Centred Approach to Multilevel Governance' (Paper presented at the APSA meeting, San Francisco, 29 August–1 September 1996).

Marks, G., L. Hooghe and K. Blank
    1996   'European Integration from the 1980s: State-Centric v Multi-Level Governance', *Journal of Common Market Studies* 34.3: 341-78.

Marsh, D., and R.A.W. Rhodes
    1992   'Policy Communities and Issue Networks: Beyond Typology', in Marsh and Rhodes (eds.) 1992: 249-68.

Marsh, D., and R.A.W. Rhodes (eds.)
    1992   *Policy Networks in British Government* (Oxford: Oxford University Press).

Martin, S., and Pearce, G.
    1993   'European Regional Development Strategies: Strengthening Meso-Gov-
                ernment in the UK?', *Regional Studies* 27.7: 682-96.

Martins, M., and J. Mawson
    1980a   'The Evolution of EEC Regional Policy: Cosmetics or Major Surgery?',
                Local Government Studies, July/August 1980: 29-55.
    1980b   'Regional Trends in the European Community and the Revision of the
                Common Regional Policy', *Built Environment* 6.2: 145-52.
    1982   'The Programming of Regional Development in the EC: Supranational or
                International Decision-Making?', *Journal of Common Market Studies*
                20.3: 229-44.
    1983   'The Development of the "Programme Approach" in the Common
                Regional Policy: An Evaluation of the British Experience', *Town Plan-
                ning Review* 54.1: 63-82.

Mawson, J., M. Martins and J. Gibney
    1985   'The Development of the European Community Regional Policy', in
                Keating and Jones (eds.) 1985: 20-59.

Mazey, S., and J. Richardson
    1993   'Policy Co-ordination in Brussels: Environmental and Regional Policy'
                (European Public Policy Institute, Occasional Papers, 93/5; Warwick:
                University of Warwick).

McAleavey, P.
    1992   'The Politics of European Regional Development Policy: The European
                Commission's RECHAR Initiative and the Concept of Additionality'
                (Strathclyde Papers on Government and Politics, 88; Glasgow: University
                of Strathclyde).
    1993   'The Politics of the European Regional Development Policy: Additional-
                ity in the Scottish Coalfields', *Regional Politics and Policy* 3.2: 88-107.
    1994   'The Political Logic of the European Community Structural Funds
                Budget: Lobbying Efforts by Declining Industrial Regions' (EUI Work-
                ing Paper RSC, 94.2; Florence: European University Institute, Robert
                Schuman Centre, Badia Fiesolana, San Domenico [FI]).
    1995a   'Policy Implementation as Incomplete Contracting: The European
                Regional Development Fund' (Unpublished PhD thesis; Florence: Euro-
                pean University Institute).
    1995b   'European Regional Development Fund Expenditure in the UK: From
                Additionality to Subtractionality', *European Urban and Regional Studies*
                2.3: 249-53.

Meny, Y.
    1982   'Should the Community Regional Policy Be Scrapped?', *Common
                Market Law Review* 19.3: 373-88.

Millan, B.
    1992   Letter in reply to Sir John Kerr (see above) from Bruce Millan, Commis-
                sioner for Regional Policy, 13 February 1992.

Morata, F., and X. Munoz
    1996   'Vying for European Funds: Territorial Restructuring in Spain', in
                Hooghe (ed.) 1996: 195-214.

Moravcsik, A.
   1991   'Negotiating the Single European Act', in Keohane and Hoffmann (eds.)
             1991: 41-84.
   1993   'Preferences and Power in the European Community: A Liberal Inter-
             governmentalist Approach', *Journal of Common Market Studies* 31.4:
             473-519.
   1995   'Liberal Intergovernmentalism and Integration: A Rejoinder', *Journal of
             Common Market Studies* 33. 4: 611-28.
Moxon-Browne, E.
   1993   'Social Europe', in Lodge (ed.) 1993: 152-63.
Mutti, A.
   1990   'The Role of Trust in Political Exchange', in B. Marin (ed.), *Generalized
             Political Exchange: Antagonistic Cooperation and Integrated Policy Cir-
             cuits* (Frankfurt am Main: Campus Verlag): 199-214.
Nanetti, R.
   1996   'EU Cohesion and Territorial Restructuring in the Member States', in
             Hooghe (ed.) 1996: 59-88.
NIERC
   1992   'European Community Structural Funds in Northern Ireland' (Report by
             the Northern Ireland Economic Research Council, 94; Belfast: Northern
             Ireland Economic Development Office, April 1992).
Official Journal of the European Communities
   1988a   Council Regulation (EEC) No 2052/88, on the tasks of the Structural
             Funds and their effectiveness and on coordination of their activities
             between themselves and with the operations of the European Investment
             Bank and the other existing financial instruments, 24 June 1988.
   1988b   Council Regulation (EEC) No 4254/88, laying down provisions for
             implementing Regulation (EEC) No 2052/88 as regards the European
             Regional Development Fund, 19 December 1988.
   1988c   Legislation, L374, Volume 31, 31 December 1988.
Page, E., and M. Goldsmith (eds.)
   1987   *Central and Local Government Relations; A Comparative Analysis of
             West European Unitary States* (London: Sage).
Peters, B.G.
   1992   'Bureaucratic Politics and the Institutions of the European Community',
             in Sbragia (ed.) 1992: 75-122.
Peterson, J.
   1992   'The European Technology Community: Policy Networks in a Supra-
             national Setting', in Marsh and Rhodes (eds.) 1992.
   1995a   'Decision-Making in the European Union: Towards a Framework for
             Analysis', *Journal of European Public Policy* 2.1: 69-93.
   1995b   'EU Research Policy: The Politics of Expertise', in Rhodes and Mazey
             (eds.) 1995: 391-412
Peterson, J., and Bomberg, E.
   1993   'Decision Making in the European Union: A Policy Networks Approach'
             (Prepared for presentation to the annual conference of the UK Political
             Studies Association, Leicester, 20–22 April 1993).

Pillinger, J.
    1992   'Social Partner Participation in the Operation of the European Structural Funds in the United Kingdom: The North West of England' (Report to the European Commission; Barnsley: Northern College).

    1994   *The European Structural Funds: Final Report of the Evidence Submitted to the UK Hearings* (Barnsley: Northern College).

Pinder, D.
    1983   *Regional Economic Development Policy: Theory and Practice in the European Community* (London: George Allen & Unwin).

Pollack, M.
    1995   'Regional Actors in an Intergovernmental Play: The Making and Implementation of EC Structural Policy', in Rhodes and Mazey (eds.) 1995: 361-90.

    1996   'The New Institutionalism and EC Governance: The Promise and Limits of Institutional Analysis', *Governance* 9.4: 429-58.

Preston, C.
    1983   'Additional to What? Does the U.K. Government Cheat on the European Regional Development Fund?', *Politics* 3.2: 20-26.

    1984   'The Politics of Implementation: The European Community Regional Development Fund and European Community Regional Aid to the UK 1975–81' (Unpublished PhD thesis; University of Essex).

Putnam, R.D.
    1988   'Diplomacy and Domestic Politics: The Logic of Two Level Games', *International Organization* 42.3: 427-60.

    1993   *Making Democracy Work: Civic Traditions in Modern Italy* (Princeton, NJ: Princeton University Press).

Rhodes, C., and S. Mazey (eds.)
    1995   *The State of the European Union. III. Building a European Polity?* (Boulder, CO: Lynne Riener; Harlow: Longman).

Rhodes, R.A.W.
    1981   *Control and Power in Central–Local Relations* (Aldershot: Gower).

    1986a   *The National World of Local Government* (London: Allen & Unwin).

    1986b   ' "Power Dependence" Theories of Central–Local Relations: A Critical Assessment', in Goldsmith (ed.) 1986: 1-36.

    1986c   *European Policy-Making, Implementation and Subcentral Governments: A Survey* (Maastricht: European Institute of Public Administration).

    1988   *Beyond Westminster and Whitehall* (London: Unwin–Hyman).

    1992   *The Europeanization of Sub-Central Government: The Case of the UK, Staatswissenschaften und Staatspraxis* (Baden-Baden: Nomos Verlagsgesellschaft).

    1995   'The New Governance: Governing without Government', *The State of Britain, Seminar 2* (Swindon: ESRC).

    1996   'Governing without Government: Order and Change in British Politics' (Inaugural lecture, Newcastle University, 18 April 1996).

    1997   *Understanding Governance: Policy Networks, Reflexivity and Accountability* (Buckingham, PA: Open University Press).

Rhodes, R.A.W., I. Bache and S. George
    1996   'Policy Networks and Policy-Making in the European Union: A Critical
              Appraisal', in Hooghe (ed.) 1996: 367-87.
Rhodes, R.A.W., and D. Marsh
    1992   'Policy Networks on British Politics: A Critique of Existing Approaches',
              in Marsh and Rhodes (eds.) 1992: 1-26.
Richardson, J.
    1993   'Actor Based Models of National and EU Policy Making: Policy Com-
              munities, Issue Networks and Epistemic Communities' (Paper presented
              to the ESRC's seminar series, 'The Impact of EC Action on National
              Policy and Policy Making in Industrial, Financial and Service Sectors',
              University of Oxford, 10–11 December 1993).
Richardson, J.J., and A.G. Jordan
    1979   *Governing under Pressure: The Policy Process in a Post-Parliamentary
              Democracy* (Oxford: Martin Robertson).
Risse-Kappen, T.
    1996   'Exploring the Nature of the Beast: International Relations Theory and
              Comparative Policy Analysis Meet the European Union', *Journal of
              Common Market Studies* 34.1: 53-80.
Salt, Cllr H.
    1992   'ERDF Grants and the Additionality Problem' (Letter to the ACC, ADC,
              AMA and COSLA from the Chair of the Coalfield Communities Cam-
              paign, 7 October 1992).
Sandholtz, W., and J. Zysman
    1989   '1992: Recasting the European Bargain', *World Politics* 42: 95-128.
Sbragia, A. (ed.)
    1992   *Euro-Politics: Institutions and Policymaking in the 'New' European
              Community* (Washington, DC: Brookings Institution).
Scott, J.
    1995   *Development Dilemmas in the European Community: Rethinking Region-
              al Development Policy* (Buckingham/Philadelphia: Open University
              Press).
    1998   'Law, Legitimacy and EC Governance: Prospects for "Partnership" ',
              Journal of Common Market Studies 36.2.
    1999   'Regional Policy: An Evolutionary Perspective', in P.P. Craig and G. de
              Búrca, *An Evolutionary Perspective on EU Law* (Oxford: Oxford Univer-
              sity Press).
Stoker, G.
    1995   'Intergovernmental Relations', *Public Administration* 73: 101-22.
    1997   *Local Political Participation: New Perspectives on Local Governance*
              (York: Joseph Rowntree Foundation).
Swift, M.
    1978   'A Regional Policy for Europe', *Young Fabian Pamphlet* 48 (London:
              Fabian Society).
Thomas, I.
    1992   'Additionality in the Distribution of European Regional Development
              Fund Grants to Local Authorities', *Local Economy* 6.4: 292-310.

Tofarides, M.
    1997   'Cities and the European Union: An Unforeseen Alliance?' (The European Policy Process, Occasional Paper, 30; Florence: European University Institute).
    forthcoming 'The Multi-Level Gatekeeper System: The Case of the European Union's Urban Policy Experiment' (PhD thesis; Florence: European University Institute).
Tranholm-Mikkelsen, J.
    1991   'Neofunctionalism: Obstinate or Obsolete? A Reappraisal in the Light of the New Dynamism of the European Community', *Millennium* 20: 1-22.
Vanhove, K., and L.H. Klaassen
    1987   *Regional Policy: A European Approach* (Aldershot: Gower, 2nd edn).
Wallace, H.
    1973   *National Governments and the European Communities* (London: Chatham House/PEP).
    1977a   'National Bulls in the Community China Shop: The Role of National Governments in Community Policy-Making', in Wallace, Wallace and Webb (eds.) 1977: 33-68.
    1977b   'The Establishment of the Regional Development Fund: Common Policy or Pork Barrel?', in Wallace, Wallace and Webb (eds.) 1977: 137-63.
    1980   *Budgetary Politics: The Finances of the European Communities* (London: George Allen).
    1983a   'Negotiation, Conflict and Compromise: The Elusive Pursuit of Common Policies', in Wallace, Wallace and Webb (eds.) 1983 43-80.
    1983b   'Distributional Politics: Dividing up the Community Cake', in Wallace, Wallace and Webb (eds.) 1983: 81-113.
Wallace, H., and W. Wallace
    1996   *Policy-Making in the European Union* (Oxford: Oxford University Press, 3rd edn).
Wallace, H., W. Wallace and C. Webb (eds.)
    1977   *Policy-Making in the European Communities* (London: John Wiley).
    1983   *Policy-Making in the European Communities* (London: John Wiley, 2nd edn).
Wallace, W.
    1983   'Less than a Federation, More than a Regime: The Community as a Political System', in Wallace, Wallace and Webb (eds.) 1983: 403-36.
Wallace, W., and H. Wallace
    1990   'Strong State or Weak State in Foreign Policy? The Contradictions of Conservative Liberalism, 1979–1987', *Public Administration* 68: 83-101.
Watson, R.
    1998   'Sweetening the Bitter Pill of Budget Consolidation', *European Voice*, 26 March–1 April 1998: 16.
Webb, C.
    1983   'Theoretical Perspectives and Problems', in Wallace, Wallace and Webb (eds.) 1983: 1-42.
Welfare, D., and K. Beaumont
    1993b   'Additionality: The Key to Understanding it', *Municipal Review and*

            AMA News 743 (London: Association of Metropolitan Authorities,
            December 1993): 182-83.
Williams, K., J. Williams and C. Haslam
    1991   'What Kind of Regional Policy?', *Local Economy* 5.4 (1991): 330-46.
Wilson, J.
    1980   'The European Community's Regional Policy', *Local Government
            Studies*, July/August: 11-28.
Wincott, D.
    1995   'Institutional Interaction and European Integration: Towards an Everyday
            Critique of Liberal Intergovernmentalism', *Journal of Common Market
            Studies* 33. 4: 597-609.
Wise, M., and G. Croxford
    1988   'The European Regional Development Fund: Community Ideals and
            National Realities', *Political Geography Quarterly* 7.2: 161-82.
Wishlade, F.
    1996   'EU Cohesion Policy: Facts, Figures, and Issues', in Hooghe (ed.) 1996:
            27-58.
Wulf-Mathies, M.
    1997   'Social and Economic Cohesion in Europe: Implications for Britain'
            (Speech by the Commissioner for Regional Policy, organised by the
            Centre for European Reform, London, 27 January 1997;
            http://europa.eu.int/en/comm/dg16/key/s970127e.htm).
Yuill, D., K. Allen, J. Bachtler, K. Clement and F. Wishlade
    1991   *European Regional Incentives* (European Policies Research Centre, Uni-
            versity of Strathclyde, 11th edn; London: Bowker-Saur).

INDEX OF AUTHORS

UNIVERSITY ASSOCIATION FOR CONTEMPORARY EUROPEAN STUDIES
UACES Secretariat, King's College London, Strand, London WC2R 2LS
Tel: 0171 240 0206 Fax: 0171 836 2350 E-mail: uaces@compuserve.com
http://www.uaces.org/u-info/

UACES

University Association for Contemporary European Studies

THE ASSOCIATION

- Brings together academics involved in researching Europe with representatives of government, industry and the media who are active in European affairs
- Primary organisation for British academics researching the European Union
- Over 500 individual and corporate members from Dept such as Politics, Law, Economics & European Studies, plus a growing number of Graduate Students who join as Associate Members

MEMBERSHIP BENEFITS

- Individual Members eligible for special highly reduced fee for The Journal of Common Market Studies
- Regular Newsletter - events and developments of relevance to members
- Conferences - variety of themes, modestly priced, further reductions for members
- Publications, including the new series *Contemporary European Studies*, from May 1998
- Research Network, and research conference
- Through the European Community Studies Association (ECSA), access to a larger world wide network
- Information Documentation & Resources eg: The Register of Courses in European Studies and the Register of Research into European Integration

Current Cost of Membership per annum - Individual Members - £20.00; Graduate Students £10.00; Corporate Members £40.00 (2 copies of documentation sent and any 2 members of Dept / Organisation eligible to attend conferences at Members' rate)

APPLICATION FOR MEMBERSHIP OF UACES	BANKER'S ORDER FORM
Please indicate if you wish to receive details of the JCMS ☐	Please return to UACES and not to your Bank
I enclose Banker's Order / cheque for £ _____ payable to UACES	TO_____(Bank)
Name _____	_____ (Sort Code)
Faculty / Dept _____	AT _____(Address)
Institution _____	_____
Address _____	Please pay to Lloyds Bank (30-00-08), Pall Mall Branch, 3-10 Waterloo Place London SW1Y 4BE
_____	in favour of UACES Account No 3781242
Tel No: _____	on the _____day of _____
Fax No: _____	the sum of £20 (TWENTY POUNDS) and the same sum on the same date each year until countermanded
E-mail: _____	Signature & Date _____ _____
Signature & Date _____	Account No _____
Address for correspondence if different:	Name _____
_____	Address _____
_____	_____